D0873712

by Nancy Boutilier

According to Her Contours (1992)
On the Eighth Day Adam Slept Alone: New Poems (2000)

NANCY BOUTILIER

ON THE EIGHTH DAY ADAM SLEPT ALONE

NEW POEMS

BLACK SPARROW PRESS • SANTA ROSA • 2000

ACKNOWLEDGMENTS

Earlier versions of some of these poems first appeared in the following periodicals and anthologies: *Beyond Definition, Buckle &, The Bulletin* and *Vox.*

All philopoem definitions are adapted from the Third Edition of *The New York Public Library Desk Reference*, published by Macmillan, 1998.

Black Sparrow Press books are printed on acid-free paper.

LIBRARY OF CONGRESS CATALOGING-IN-PUBLICATION DATA

Boutilier, Nancy, 1961–
    On the eighth day Adam slept alone : new poems / Nancy Boutilier.
      p. cm.
    ISBN 1-57423-132-4 (paperback)
    ISBN 1-57423-133-2 (cloth trade)
    ISBN 1-57423-134-0 (signed cloth)
     I. Title.
    PS3552. O8364 O5   2000
    811'.54—dc21   00-29742

This collection of poems
is dedicated to my grandmother,
Elsie Wyman Kallgren,
who let me turn the pages
as she read me my first Dr. Seuss.
Gram, I know how you love to read biographies—
these words are my life,
but don't worry,
I make up all the parts
that are true.

Contents

ON THE EIGHTH DAY ADAM SLEPT ALONE

New Poems

I. LOYALTY

Allegiances

Empiricism: *knowledge derives from
experience or sensation rather than from
reason.*

so she returned to her father's house without an
ax or even a gun. she kissed everyone at the door,
dared to hold her father for a second longer than
the others. her mother looked on with reasons of
her own. the bread was forgotten in the oven.

Journeying to My Deepest Before

She is not
the one
I love
but

the pull of her chin
the bend of her lip
the curl of her steady grin
ring with something

so familiar
so remembered
so distant
so longed for

that I am mesmerized
by a conversation
I do not
hear.

As the lingerings
in the margins of her face
outshine the words
formed by her mouth

unsounding syllables
buzz off her tongue
sonic waves
slip past teeth

and journey to my deepest before
only to return with a beep and a blip on some unseen screen in me,
as if locating my outlying planets,
my invisible outposts, the depths of my ocean floor.

Though she started only
as reflection,
like a shadow

she has stretched beyond her original form,

an echo
emerging
independent from its source,
a sound in her own right.

And tonight I relish
every note, every stir
formed and reflected
by the movement of her familiar mouth.

Uprooted

Deep voices crack static:

                  Scratchy   beeps   and blips

        salt   and   pepper

                my   dreamy   state

Huddled with me on the couch
my parents prodding me
awake
past bedtime

              I am eight and feeling
              big
              enough to watch
              the late night broadcast

Everyone has told me
how historic
how meaningful
this is

        And there
        on television
        bundled   bubbled   bouncing

                            are Neil and Buzz

Tomorrow on the playground
we will play their parts
and recite a litany of code words
One small step for man   *Roger*   *Over and Out*   *We read you*

But tonight far away   on a dark cratered desert
two men own an alien playground   hit a few loopy rounds of golf
raise a flag   to stake their claim
and dance   a nation's dream

More than the distant moon
Earth
suspended behind the slow-moving men
captures my attention

To see that gaseous disc   glow on the horizon
                                        and grow into a lighted globe
stirs something unfrightenable
                          in me

              So more whole
              unknowable
              unownable
              the world appears now

              Than when I have held it in my hands
              given it a spin on thin metal axis
              all in all no bigger than a basketball
              atop the teacher's desk

              What a lie it was
              to let me   trace   my fingers   over
              countries   patched together
              in jigsaw puzzle shapes

Those colors on maps and globes   seem so unearthly now
trying to demarcate that which   we divide
and claim   to know
continents   states   oceans   lakes   poles

Like honesty looming behind the weightless men
                                              Earth hangs so still
punctuating the sky
            dotting the cosmic question mark

                                     Earth hangs
so unlike maps that find themselves pinned up
            like centerfolds
                       as if controlled by those who place the tacks

                                  This Earth I see
on TV defies the blues and greens and browns claiming to establish
      boundaries
the silly contour lines
      the very metaphor of mapping

                You couldn't fold it away
                in a glove compartment
                or find its road
                to Mandalay

                            This earth
                   perches in
                         darkness
                         so perfectly   alive

As if the very source
            of light flickering
                  across the snowy screen
                        of our old Zenith.

Earth smooth
and round
and marbled   blue and white
                         so still

So vast

so regal

and so far

away

Until an instant of understanding
spins me on my own tiny axis
in realization
that somewhere   on that shining ark   is me

Tiny traveler
that I am
held in its floating folds
orbiting the galaxies

And feeling

small

so small

so small

Even at eight
staying up late to witness history
via satellite   I knew I had seen

the answer

To some question
not
yet
found

And now
after all these years
with so many questions
spinning me

The answer
has slipped away
and hidden itself
in the stars.

Patriotism on Sunset Drive

The Fourth of July of my childhood
was a neighborhood
parade designed
I am now sure
as an excuse for parents
to supervise
our fireworks.
Bottle rockets
cherry bombs
and M-80s
smuggled over safe borders
when returning from
Florida or
Niagara Falls.
Enough for the whole street to share.
And I am there
on Independence Day
in a tiny square photograph
my five-year-old self
in a tri-cornered hat
riding a rocking horse
mounted in a red wagon.
As my favorite minuteman
Paul Revere
I make my historic ride
down Sunset Drive
as Grandpa pulls me along.
We both wave to
my mother's Instamatic.
Had video been in fashion
we would have more
than a snapshot today,
perhaps audio evidence
of my patriot cry:
"The British are coming!"
"The British are coming!"

> (Elsewhere streets were filled with marchers
> who had other revolutionary cries. I knew

nothing of the tear gas, lynch mobs, or riot
squads they faced. Acid trips, flower power,
rock 'n' roll were outlawed in my little
town. I overheard someone call my baby-
sitter's brother a hippie, something about
his hair, not eating meat, and living on a
commune. There were occasional whispers
about draft dodging, school busing, and the
Jews but I knew little of patriots who wore
stripes other than my own, who pledged
allegiance to change, who set the flag to
flames.)

Year by year
through the sixties
we'd gather
for our solemn ceremonies
on The Fourth
in the circle of our sleepy
dead end street.
Dad put on a top hat
and seersucker coat
to play Uncle Sam—
though often I confused him
with Abe Lincoln.
Dad stood center stage
with me solemnly beside him
and a half-step behind
as he recited what must have been
the Declaration one year
the Emancipation Proclamation the next.
But what remains clearest
and most red, white and blue
in my mind is the story
Dad told about a champion
bullfrog.
His animated telling of the tale
convinced me that Mark Twain
must have been a founding father too.
I delighted in knowing
that cleverness and cunning
not only defeated the unbeatable frog,

but also helped to get the country running.
After all, I knew the secret
to each sleight of hand
behind Dad's show of sorcery.
I knew Uncle Sam's little magic tricks:
the flash powder
that made fingers burst to flame;
the slippery move that let the coin
appear to pass in one ear and out the other
right through my brother's crew-cut brain;
the mystical pitcher Dad used
to pour the milk into his silk top hat.
Then, with one abra-ca-dabra wave
and to everyone's amazement
he brought forth daisies!
There was no talk of Cambodia
or Montgomery,
just our humble Pledge of Allegiance
and sparklers for everyone.
You could have convinced me that Kent State
was the 51st—after Hawaii and Alaska, that is.
Joanie's father swallowed fire
and Mr. Barney wore his uniform and medals.
I took patriotic pride
in knowing that Dad was Uncle Sam
that his magic was really
just an act—
an art
of deception.
It was patriotism
I suppose.
A love of home.
Flags flew
Hot dogs grilled.
Firecrackers blasted.
It was a way to love
one's country.

Nude Descending a Soapbox

It was hard to take her seriously.
The issues were real
I know
but so was the show of thigh
    the smooth swagger of hips
        the ripple of tender tissue as it flexed
            and unflexed before the listening eye.

She had a point to make
strong arguments too
but she had curves
that flashed in the afternoon light
    and a bend in her back
        that took three beats
            out of the heart's every four.

She aroused with her conviction
entertained with her wit
and reasoned soundly
but as the nude stepped down from her soapbox
    the utterance of her flesh
        the parlance of her posture
            the two pronouncements of her breasts

spoke with a diction that was far more convincing
than any jargon rhetorical.
In the end
it was the appeal
    of the succulent spaces
        that shaped her ankles
        that lasted

and left one believing
that no lifetime would be wasted
in pursuit of her out-takes
on a quest for the mysteries of and beyond her flesh.
    Sometimes the only available hold is language.

The body begs translation
of what words approximate

because the meaning of things said
and unsaid
like the line
of her neck
    is exactly
            what renders one satisfied
                and speechless.

Snapper AFGUE

stick
long as a sneaker
thick as a penny
clapped folded
snapped   in half
by the trap of the turtle's jaw

could have been a thumb
but it wasn't
could have made me sick
to my stomach
but it didn't   only curiosity bit

"Let's try to catch one."
    You nuts?
"We can make a hundred dollars."
    No way…   *How?*
"White Cliffs serves turtle soup, ya know."
    No way.
"Yes way. Haven't you seen the sign? It says FINE DINING."

              the swamp
shaggy water stagnant tadpoles canada geese polliwogs black ice
that cracked early in winter bullfrogs algae fights in summer (a
snapper somewhere) waterbugs rafts built of wood stolen from
construction sites mom's voice cutting through the woods time to
head home for dinner muddy sneakers wet dog following

"Hey, Dad. Isn't there such thing as turtle soup?"

morning oatmeal
refill of juice gives me a chance to steal bait (cheese and sliced ham)

—What do you kids have planned for today?

"Nothing. Just hang out, I guess."
        1. Meet at Camelot (the third fort built that summer)

2. Collect our "gear" (old high tops that can't be sucked off
        your heels in mud, cigarettes, matches, slingshots, a tin
        of Copenhagen, firecrackers—in case we find frogs—
        and long bamboo poles to propel the rafts)
   3. Head for The Shipyard (a small marshy corner of The
        Swamp where we kept The Fleet AFGUE—A F G U E,
        acronym acting as an adverb: Away From Grown Up
        Eyes)

Later that morning:
        "One or two?"
"Two. You take *The Chipmunk* and I'll take the *USS Prostitution.*"

poled our way to open water
chose our sectors
promise to signal (ca-hoo, ca-hoo)
if we struck turtle

pole glide poke squish swish plop   sun rising shining off thick
soup shaggy water pole poke   logs tease with their hard surface
awakening eager hunters to the possibility of a snapper's shell
eyes narrow to a squint   water heats up with day   croaking quiets
ducks resting in shade   sweat stings   algae tangles pole tug slip
feet wet cool   waterbugs skate on surface   back bakes   a bark
intrudes from up the hill   rafts coast poles push prod soft sticky
gush slide goo mud push pole glide

"Anything for you?"
        Not yet. You?
"Nope. Lunch?"
        You sure we can make one hundred dollars?
"Yup." (I was.)
        OK. Where do you want to dock?

Inlet
shade
allows only one port
dock end-to-end
first *The Chipmunk* then *The Prostitution* both of us stand
together on the 1-man (smaller of the two rafts) *Chipmunk,*
submerging

two girls on a 1-man sink ankle deep
murk seeps
        then floods sneakers
                algae creeps and slithers on skinny shins
                        water so dark
            little to see
                        below the knee
        momentarily
                    the raft becomes a submarine
    that we stand atop   without a periscope.

The first leaps off and
                    raft lurches
                            underwater

one safe on the leafy shore   the other remains on deck as raft rises

eyes bigger than bullfrogs
                            raft surfaces
no time to say ca-hoo ca-hoo
                call me Ishmael   eye to eye with our hundred dollar
hunt

    gather   acorns

    load   slingshot

        aim
        aim
        take
        in
        air
        aim
        &
        fire
                                    acorn

                    ricochets
                                    off knobby
                shell

| 30

no mark
        no movement
                    no moan

reload   slingshot
        pull   band
            back further
            for
            deadlier
            shot
            aim
            lower
            note paws
            not feet
            but stumps
            scaly
            limbs
            thick
            knotted
            logs
            with claws
            and jaw
            that jaw
            jaw jaw
            horny lip jaw
            spiking down
            like some reptilian
                    stalactite
                    a beak
                    that could
                    break
                    bones

                    breathe
                    aim
                    again
                    take
                    in
                    air
                    aim

31

Memory of Grandpa's voice: *Eyes. The eyes. Before you shoot, look 'er in the eyes.*
                         The eyes
                         wild stare
                         no squint
                         no glare
                         defiant

Another voice, younger and closer:
   "It's not moving. Do you think it's dead or maybe playing dead? Possums do."

toss some bait   ("Maybe they don't like cheese.")
toss the ham   ("Maybe it's not hungry.")
slight pole poke   (nothing)
poke prod push gentle first then harder (no blink no snap no movement)

   "Even a possum woulda run by now."

One last thrill rafting our kill
                        (that we didn't have to kill)
                                           back to base:

the creeping in of fear (and hope?) that some magical mix of wind and water skimming along the swampy surface would seep in to those turtle lungs and resurrect a sleepy memory of swimming breathing snapping living … it didn't. the snapper never moved.

snow shovel lifts turtle to red wagon lined with wet towels and ice
thermos full of Tang   three-mile walk to White Cliffs restaurant
front door: knock knock knock / locked / around to service entrance:

                                           "Turtle soup? Is this some kind
                                         of joke. No. What? For God's
                                         sake, get that thing out of here!
                                         Get it out. Do you want me to
                                         call the cops?!"

                   without words
                   we stopped
                   not far away
                   in a shaded spot
                   by the side of the road

best hole we could muster
with a snow shovel
gentle with the turtle
"should we say prayer?"
We didn't   (but maybe I did).

Finding Comfort in Patterns

There is a comfort in patterns, even
bad habits bring familiar ease.
Why is it that this rhythm soothes what no
words can achieve? To feel is so much more real
than to think or to say what is true.
The old dog who won't learn a single new trick.

The masks that you wear still trick
me into believing that even
at this late date you can change, turn true.
Perhaps I can adapt, find a way to ease
the spin that sends me into a crippling reel.
I just want our lives to be safe between these cracked walls, but no.

There is no
calling the bluff, revealing the trick
of our stacked deck, your unsteady deal, not when the real
you needs the last word or even
more. Some would call it a disease,
what you and I have, but I don't want that to be true.

There's no way to construe
a cure or even relief. Sleep brings no
rest. If only I could appease
you or please you or trick
you into a more even
temper, then the love that we call ours would be real.

But how can one measure what is real
or true
in an uneven
world? Are we walking on eggs or just their shells? No
one has offered me a bag of tricks
or a magic bullet. How does one ease

the sag of life? Something breaks with each easy
step, and all I want is a final chapter that offers real
release, a light at the end of this grave. Then no tricks

would be needed to find the true,
the tender, the world in which no
body suffers, nobody else gets hurt, not even

me. It's easy to think or believe that no-
thing is real—not the house, not the scars, not the hole in the wall,
        not even
my own imagination is playing this trick on me: you are too good
        to be true.

I Used to Write Sunrises

I used to write
sunrises.
A new day yawning
peaceful and majestic
reflected in the still pool
outside an extravagant tomb
or the summer solstice
waking up with me
stretching
to the gentle tune
of leaf on leaf.
Every day
that same sun
ever promising
another new beginning
stepping off the top step
of red rock walls
hurdling high-rises
Aphrodite, emerging from the foam
to mount the sky
to oversee another day.
In places wide and narrow
dust and stone
lush and scorched
I have felt myself alive
and strong
while escorting in
another dawn
another today
another wave
on the crest of
another tomorrow.

Now I write sunsets
only sunsets
I see them everywhere
that final terrific blaze
disappearing

into the jaws of a hot horizon
a tear dropping
over the distant ledge of the Pacific.
I climb peaks
to see
those last bright rays
sink behind the skyline
tuck away into the clouds
drop beyond the Bay.

Every bird was flying
east tonight.
To the west
the red sky grew thick
with fog
and dim.
I thought I saw your lovely ghost
but it was just the sun
falling
once
again
off this lonely coast.

Help Arrives

there won't always be a glass to break
an alarm to pull
or even a rope
at the other end

help arrives
on its own wings

a slice of light
a familiar rhythm
a word discovered
or rediscovered

crisis always ends
but resolution
is not the same as
solution

a stillness
a cure
a departure
longing and belonging

there won't always be answers
to questions
prayers
or cries

for help
no bell to ring
no buzzer to sound
no marines to send in

no buoy to throw
no ladder to extend
no rest
no rescue

only stillness
the reliability of light
a word
touch

sleep
memory
release
need

but help arrives
on its own
wings
mercy too

as if there
was never
any
doubt

Closure

He might have known what to do with a kid
brother, but the sister in his footsteps wanted
answers to questions she trembled to ask. He
masked love so deliciously in slap shots and
hip checks that she did not notice how
affectionately he elbowed her in the
ribs to tell her that she could
tag along only if she kept
silent.

How silent
her tag
screaming in blue paint between the ribs
of the bridge over the Charles, affectionately.
Graffiti is hip
she thought to herself, knowing that the she had unmasked
her love and loss like the answers
to riddles her brother
would never know, if only he

II. INTENTION

Accidents

Nominalism: *ideas and objects exist only in the particular instance not as abstract concepts. All universals are merely names and have no existence on their own.*

no pain is unbearable. passing out is just a different way to bear it. would I continue swinging even after she was down? would we pull hair or use our teeth? could she sink me with a blind-sider to the brow? how damaging is my hook? could I take her out with an uppercut unseen? perhaps a flurry of disingenuous jabs until one of us delivered the unanswerable blow. I imagine a knockout punch knowing that anger cannot fly without the wings I give it.

New Math

She wanted life to come
with the answers
at the back
of the book.
She longed for calculus
to aid her in cutting her hair
for trigonometry to solve world hunger
but the geometry of it all
made her shiver
and the arc of her palm
tasted more and more
triangular each day
until she could
no longer recognize even
numbers or the odd face
in the three-way mirror.
She set out in new directions
looking for light that would fall
on her shoes
without tripping her.
What a journey it was
through that maze
of questions
with answers
she did not want.
In her dreams
she understood
what the snakes
needed to stop
their hissing
but she was
too busy
kissing
her best friend
from grade school
to bother with them.

To be an angel

is to dive-bomb with
gulls who have
nowhere to perch.

Back in her dreams
she lost track of time
arriving too late
to solve the equation.
The shoeless lady
with the lopsided hair
begged her for money
to feed the cat that purred quietly in her lap.
Children with whiskers and tiny paws
gave her presents of string and ribbon
whispering words that deserved new meanings—
distress, diatribe, and *humpty-dumpty.*

The brittle streets
cracked under her footsteps
and the moon barked
a little brightness that
made all the shadows hide
under the tongues of prophets.
Oh, when will the sages remember
the dangers
of landing?
"Are you a boy or a man?"
someone asked
and she did not know
how to answer.
THIS WAY OUT blinked
the big pink sign
but she turned her back
on neon; it pointed to nowhere
new. "I won't be your fool"
she said to herself
(though she did not know
how to respond
to her own demands).
But the textbooks
and their technicians

were eavesdropping
long enough to echo back at her
in Esperanto
telling her what she already knew:
we're all fools
in one language or another.

This Will Not Be Political

If cows resemble government
officials in your region
I'm sorry.
If rainbows call up the wicked witch of the west
and munchkins
then blame Hollywood.
If a banana takes a Freudian turn
your mind gives it that bend
not my poem.

> The rainbow arched like a banana
> confusing the cow and
> tripping her up
> as she made
> her way
> over the
> steady
> moon.

What Holds

When I see you now, I think of the second
my eyes first fell upon your smile, and I must
admit that time
froze in that moment, a sign
of something yet to come
or something broken

or both. When a child's first baseball mitt is broken
in, there grows a hope that a second
player will soon come
and make two for a game of catch. You must
have flashed the fast ball sign
to yourself, playing both pitcher and catcher at one time.

Resorting to pop flies after a time
playing in the backyard next to a broken
swing set, you pretended to sign
autographs for admiring fans as star second
baseman in the big leagues. What must
you do to turn a double play once try-outs come?

Those games are long behind us, but come
let us remember time
as we wish it. Life must
have been sweet before broken
in the half-light of that solid millisecond.
I did not see you coming—no warning, no signal, no sign.

I look for some reasonable design
of what is to come
and you tell me about entropy, The Second
Law, the natural demand that time
passing leads to a broken
order, all falls apart as it must.

Not the same as decay, you say, and I must
have shown some clear sign
of what was unspoken. In my unbroken

dream we hold our shapes and become
the frozen and lasting measure of time-
lessness on this turning urn, burning for an eternal second.

If I must resign myself to a broken
journey, come forward with me and let us learn to rewind time,
transforming that lost first chance into a merciful second.

When Straight Women Flirt ... with Me

She sits on my lesbian lap
both of us too much wine
arm around my shoulder
hair carelessly tossed from her face
her full weight light upon me
sweet sweat rising in the noisy night
her laugh laps up the smoke
her lean close
her breathing flirts with mine
small confessions of girlhood slumber parties spill out and
into my ear long unspoken memories
of pairing up with other girls to practice kissing
she tosses excitement of kitten innocence
in my face
roller skate caresses
first tastes of a delicious shudder

first caress and innocence innocence innocence only in a sense
implication of guilt guilt guilt
the unsaid in her sentence
she tosses excitement
her breathing breathless breathing breath breast
breasts breasts breasts oh flirt with my
around my shoulder lean close close close
both of us taste too much
too much to touch ankles thighs fingers ribs eyes ears toes
her arm my shoulder my shoulder her arm alarm disarm
dare me dare me dare me
no harm my shoulder her arm my shoulder hold her fold her
I never told her
my small confession:
I don't practice
kissing

Beyond the Sentence

Trapped in the objective singular present
and restrictive clauses, we parse our way through
a life weighted by the past
and the possessive.
Where are the plural and superlative
when you need them?
Who stole the holy tropes?
And which way will you turn
at the next conjunction?

If only hyphenation could link us
as simply as it joins names.
Will parataxis splice us together
on the page
as not in life?
How closely can we pivot
on the axis of a virgule,
that lean slash between
the either/or?

The pilcrow is often only implied.
There isn't always a simple case:
accusative, causative, reflexive.
Letters mark pages with false certainty
as if every article
were definite.
My only advice is this:
Beware redulplication.
Twice.

What I wouldn't give
to hear the cunning hiss
of a sibilant kiss
or to know
the sound of a lasting
bilabial.

Get thee to a syllabary.

Let loose the word-hoard.
Unleash the common nouns.

Only the grammarian does not lament
the insincerity of syntax:
    ambiguity sufficiently modified,
        upheaval placed properly on the page,
            and *confusion* so well-defined.

Not so in life
as it is in linguistics.
There is rarely a middle voice
to let the subject act
on or for
itself,
no fistnote
to clarify the catachresis.

When all is said, done, and written,
who wouldn't want to go out
with an everlasting interrobang?!

Wrapped as we are
in the objective singular present
we can only envy grammar
its orderliness of punctuation
the clean end
to every sentence.

Leap of Faith

A body leans before it trusts the soul.
Your reach toward me arrives with silken touch.
I'll find my limits when I lose control.

My borders long held under tight patrol.
Held captive by my proper lock and hush.
A body leans before it trusts the soul.

It is love's profit that my heart you stole.
Your rocky hide-away is warm and lush.
I'll find my limits when I lose control.

My hunger growls until you fill my bowl.
In my thick blindness, you keep careful watch.
A body leans before it trusts the soul.

So patiently you playfully cajole,
While teaching me to jump the Double Dutch.
I'll find my limits when I lose control.

I turn to you; our two halves make a whole.
Restraint unleashes in chaotic rush.
A body leans before it trusts the soul.
We'll find our limits when we lose control.

At the British Museum

I.   this stone
found devotion
to remind the goddess

in the temple
was found
placed

is mounted
its original pedestal
temple

was
the king's devotion
at the British Museum

II.   Here stands the Assyrian king
in the British Museum.
His goddess unseen.

The king would be appalled
to discover
that on his original pedestal

he stands
the center of attention
3000 years later.

Without his consent
he has abandoned
his post.

The goddess
has lost
her devotee.

Her attendant has flown the temple

taken leave of belief
skipped town.

She has been stripped
of her truest
believer.

III.   What good is the original pedestal
after centuries
of relocation?

And what of the goddess?
Where is she
without devotion?

Unseeable, unnamed,
and so undiscovered,
this once worshipped goddess,

Perhaps Tiamat,
bearer of earth
and skies,

or Mother Hubur whose two eyes
gave rise to the great rivers:
Tigris and Euphrates.

Now only the stones know
what is unknown
unheard by those gatherers of tatters and bone.

On this cold pedestal
the king stands alone
the goddesses left to the desert birds:

Siduri who dwells at the lip of the sea;
divine midwife Aruru,
and mother fate herself, Mammetum.

IV.   That rock Devotion
        unearthed from the dust
        chiseled loose from its ancient pose

        and brought to this cold cluttered corner
        of London
        to stand at attention for tourists.

V.   *This stone, which is mounted on its original pedestal*
        of reddish stone, was placed in the temple where it was found,
        to remind the goddess of the king's devotion.

VI.   Oh, Lamashtu,
        she who erases,
        hear my call.

        I am not sure who to pity most
        the king
        the deserted goddess

        or the thieves who sank
        below the level of the
        tomb they found

        who substituted
        one devotion for another
        who traded a goddess away for a dig

        Uncovering layer after
        grave layer while
        burying one king's prayer

        his final wish
        to rest
        in humble devotion

        to
        his
        goddess.

VII. What comfort is there
in a pedestal
or solid footing of any sort

when the dislocation
and the loss of intention
are so immense

that the goddess is forgotten
and the show of devotion
erased?

VIII. Nissaba,
do not abandon us
as we have abandoned you.

Though no statue stands
you have not lost
the last of your followers.

Let your milk flood and feed the fields.
Let the earth yield knowledge and grain.
What else have we to harvest?

IX. At the British Museum
the king's devotion
was

temple
its original pedestal
is mounted

placed
was found
in the temple

to remind the goddess
found devotion
this stone.

If Eskimos
have need of so many
words
for snow
then someone
somewhere
perhaps along the palm-protected shores
or amid desert winds and arid lands
has already coined a dozen words or more
to differentiate
between the various grains
of sand.

The soft loose powder
finely ground
that burns hot
and holds heat
between toes.

The grittier stuff
that moistens perfectly
when building temporary fortresses
and afternoon sand castles.

The rough stuff of vacant lots.
Sands coarse enough to
bag and buffer floods.
What a wide spectrum runs
from gravel to silt.
And dust.

Quicksand with its slow
resistance and threat.
The fine dry beads
of steady persistence
that pour out time's unyielding passage
in the hourglass.
And, alas, the soft cool comfort

of sandbox sand.

And here
along the coast
a pebbly wash
sparkles and spins
as tides drop in
and pull away
again.
Here I have spent the afternoon today
low to the water, low to the ground
sifting through the tiny stones
of mostly grays and reds and browns.

Here is where the glass hides out.
What stories the sea glass tells!
Was there once a message
in this broken bottle?
Whole did it hold homemade brew
or just a modern Mountain Dew?

Each translucent fragment
a journey.
In each shard
a life as the container and
a life as the contained.
In every glimmer of light
reflection of both solid ground
and memory of being
tossed and lost
at sea.

Each piece of glass
knows the calm of wholeness
followed by
the crash
of being shattered
and then scattered
on the waves

only to be made new

and smooth
and beautiful
again.

Here is where I spent
the entire afternoon
collecting all the sea glass I could find:
rough cut gems
tiny beach tiles
fine rounded ends
in beer-bottle browns
misty blues
porcelain whites
and crystal clears.

Sea glass—the ocean's mosaic—
magnificent in its afterlife
perfect in its broken state
shining like church windows
on the spray.

Here is where I spent half the day
and I will spend the weeks ahead
long mornings followed by entire afternoons.
Here I will grow familiar with the many kinds of sand
perhaps I will name them
as I bend and comb
this expanse by the sea
looking for the perfect cast of green
searching for a shard that I can keep
before the fog rolls in
before the next coastal storm.
I just want to hold a fragment
of the very green
I am on a quest for
the exact shade
and precise translucency.
Here at the ocean's edge
I will comb
the whole Pacific coast
for that singular green prize

for that gem of four-leaf-clover glass that I can keep
that green that holds the stories
of the deep, the lasting,
and the magic
of her eyes.

Ambulance Dreams

Another ambulance arrives
outside my house
this time bringing
the neighbor to my left
fresh oxygen.
I don't know his name
but I call him Jacob
because he's been wrestling
gods and demons for years.

At sixteen I learned to drive
and took special pride
in making way
for emergency vehicles.
I loved the wail of sirens
the prospect of rescue
the sign of hope.
Now I walk the dog of a friend
losing sight and T-cells.

The guy in 3B got a new lease
on his immune system
but his landlord showed less mercy.
When the virus finally moved in
an ambulance was called
to transport him
elsewhere.
A sign went up:
FLAT FOR RENT.

I used to comfort myself
with ambulance dreams.
On stifling summer nights
when momentary relief
from the canicular heat
was to turn the pillow to the cool side
when the fan pushed the humidity
around the room, and the dull whir

of the blades took none of the edge off the heavy air

I'd cause accidents
to soothe myself to sleep.
I'd dream up car crashes,
plane wrecks and earthquakes.
The chance to save somebody else
while my own injuries went untended.
I'd picture twisted evidence of the calamity:
doors dented, beams bent, glass shattered.
My clothes were always tattered and blood soaked.

Amid flames and choked confusion
I'd be witness to all—
pointing police to crisis
assisting rescue squads
telling the press what had happened.
Then, both victim and hero,
I would drift off to sleep
as paramedics strapped me in
and turned the ambulance toward sweet relief.

Sleep saved me
temporarily
but in my dreams
I would endure painful surgery
watch the skin bubble and blister
lose use of both hands
respond to questions with the flap of an eye
try to lift unmovable legs
as the night crawled through to morning.

I have always trained my dogs
with the strange understanding
that one day
they would fetch
my socks
bring books
to my rooted lap
answer a doorbell I could not hear
or turn on and off the water tap.

Riding a city bus
a ragged fellow with a shopping bag
filled with umbrellas
sat beside me and leaned on my shoulder.
I thought he would ask
for a dime or if I had the correct time
but he looked at me tenderly and inquired:
"Which of your past lives
do you remember?"

Not convinced
that I believed
the question,
I let him fill in my silence:
"You were blind in one life,
severely crippled in another."
Ambulances used to mark
urgency
time running out

But today's emergencies
no less disastrous
and cruel
are ongoing—
an endless string of a thousands unseen sufferings
crashless catastrophes
without rescue teams.
Ambulances have become
another form of transport.

I am still waiting
for sirens
for the chance to be calm in crisis
and then rushed away
from the messy scene to a safe
and soothing emergency room.
Perhaps we are all waiting
in urgencies of our own
to be rescued, whisked away, and finally made whole.

III. DOUBT

Dubious

Universal Doubt: *In trying to extend mathematical method to all knowledge, Descartes insisted that nothing can be considered true unless it can never be doubted under any conditions.*

Without doubt
Descartes
was never
in love.

Without God

Earth
No statement
can stand
both true
and false.

Then she tells me
"It's not about you"
and it's not.
But also it is.

Air
I tried to slit my wrist
with Ockham's razor
only to discover that it wasn't
so simple.

Fire
Pro   Con
Prosper   Consume
Prosperity   Consummation
Weighing the consequences
she starved
like the burro
who couldn't decide
between
two
equally
desirable
bales
of
hay.

Water
In a monochrome world
random acts of red
turn water
to wine.

Not Sleeping

I wish I could call up
the dreams
that swam in me
at night

I wish you could
have told me
what kept you turning
not sleeping

as I tried only to savor
the arms
that held me
at a distance

we tossed
then turned
then fell
into

sleep
and
not
sleep

Only a Test

This is a test of the Emergency Broadcasting System.
In the event of a real emergency
you will be fully informed.
This is only a test.

In the event of a real emergency
I would never leave you.
But sometimes the days grow thick with restlessness.
This is only a test.

I would never leave you.
I know you would never leave me.
But do you ever wonder who you might have been
what darkness you would have shined on if not on me?

I know you would never leave me
But when days grow slow and nights stretch across sleeplessness
you feel too far away to remain close tomorrow.
This is only a test.

Along the Canal

The city's roads bustle with bells books
and soft-skinned scholars on bicycles.
Gritty old men in scuffed blazers and flat caps
waddle along the banks of the canal
feeding swans.

Here by the cobbled bridge
a stern and stony mastiff
looks to a modern master—
the apartment complex sprouting up
in the shadow of Oxford's only castle.

This is a country of
subtleties
where birds and butterflies
go unnoticed to all
but each other.

This land of gentle green landscapes
is made jagged by towers
that spike the skies
and cathedrals crying out
for attention.

The only sharp teeth
are those of carved beasts
who populate rain spouts in courtyards,
man-made creatures invented to add dragon's fire
to a world of sleepy cattle and bleating sheep.

Every sign of heraldry
each unicorn and hippogryph
is indigenous
only to imagination,
an easy world to feel at home in.

At least until the flap of real feathers
calls this not-so-romantic Keats
back from a drunken dream world.
The ruffle of leaves and clap of wings
carries an unsinging nightingale (or was it a squab?)

                                    from one branch to another,
                                        one tree to the next.
                                In the underbrush I sit heavy
                            with how seamlessly we flow from
                                                    one town

to the next
turn from one page
to another
yearn for one love
to what?

                                    How does one move
                                            to the next
                                        without losing
                                            what came
                                            before?

The world turns.
Graduates spill through the gates.
Couples waltz by
pausing only to touch tongues
and feign a sigh.

                                    Planes fly overhead.
                                Long boats cruise past
                                stopping at Iffley Lock
                    just long enough for water levels
            to align, then on to new destinations.

The Mill Stream runs long and murky,
not deep.
Along the canal
a solitary beast
remains steady in her seat

                          locked in time and place
                     head turned to an absent master
                     obedience chiseled in her gaze
                          as the world around her
                                    shakily turns

into something unknown.
Eager and alone
stone ears open
we all await
the next command.

The Order of Emotion

There you go again
tidying up the emotions
smoothing the ro
ugh
edges
filing each feeling away alphabetically
as if A is for Anger, B for Boredom ...
You'd rack them by color too
if you knew how
                    or rank them in order of arrival.

Whose idea of survival
is this emotional
catalogue?
One book at a time—
that's Pandora's library
we are building.

Caution: time   to turn   the page.

                                        If you think this rage
                                        can be packaged
                                        arranged
                            placed carefully on a shelf
                            and locked out of sight

before the next feeling
                            looses itself
            floods the veins
stains the underwear

                            then consider
                            how
            spontaneous
                                        love
                        is
how
            whimsical

                    joy
                        HowUrgentNeed
                                    and

        how
            random
                                        ecstasy.

                                        Then
                                        consider
                                        the pluses
                                        and minuses
                                        the ins and outs
                                        the alphas and omegas
                                        of chaos
                                        add them up
                                        divide by two
                                        or by four
                                        in medias res
                                        then put away your
                                        math books
                                        your dictionaries
                                        your maps
                                        your almanacs
                                        your catalogs
                                        your index cards

                            and
            just
                    love
                                    me
    exponentially

        explosively   existentially

            exceedingly

    exquisitely

                            exhaustingly

What Remains

When does the echo become?
When does the echo become a sound in its own right?
Can what I feel in your absence be any more?
Can what I feel in your absence be any more present?
When you're right in what I feel, absence can be a sound.
Does any present become the more when in its own echo?

Was this what we came for?
Was this what we came together for?
How could I not love?
How could I not love you?
This was not how together for you
I came, what we could love.

Trace my restraint. Tell me.
Trace my restraint. Tell me your distances.
I name the parts in you that remain.
I name the parts in you that remain unnamed.
The distances trace your name. "Remain in me."
That I tell you parts my unnamed restraint.

In the echo my parts become more together
your present. Could we be sound
when what I tell you was its own trace in me?
A right love cannot name restraint,
feel any distances. This does that: how the I came for you.
Unnamed in your absence, I remain what?

Pre-Occupied

What ever happened to tenants' rights?
How did you get a key?
I used to live alone here,
but you've made a squatter out of me.

How did this shift occur?
When did it all begin?
Did you knock three times on my frontal lobe?
Did I let you in?

There must have been a lapse in judgment
or a synapse left wide open.
You slipped past my posterior root
and left no sign of break in.

I must have been out shopping
or perhaps out of the state.
You got one foot inside my cerebrum
and took over my estate.

How did you get away with it—
putting down first and last month's rent?
The lease on my brain is now in your name
but not with my consent.

You're a strain on my maxilla bone.
You snore with too much clatter.
Worst of all, your sofa
clashes with my gray matter.

I don't appreciate you leaving
my mandible unlocked.
And my pituitary gland
is no place to dry wet socks.

Your impulses—instead of mine—
win every nervous tussle.
And your parakeet keeps perching

on my orbicular muscle.

There's no room for me to sit down,
no room to dream or think.
You've been cooking in my occipital lobe,
leaving dirty dishes in the sink.

Your habits get on my cranial nerves.
Did you throw out my cerebellum?
Who said that you could smoke cigars
in my corpus callosum?

You never turn the lights out
even when nobody's home.
And you put your size-ten feet up
on my zygomatic bone.

You've monopolized my thought process.
At least you could move over!
I caught you feeding table scraps
to my favorite ganglion named Rover.

I am at my wit's end.
This is myelin, not yours.
You are in my every reflex.
You have rearranged my drawers.

When did you turn off
my entire neocortex?
Now there is no imagining
what might happen next.

My body of fornix,
you have whipped it into shape.
And who'd have known that you could give
my dura mater a new landscape?

My septum pellucidum is completely in a haze,
but what's a girl to do?
My medulla oblongata is a mess,
and I refuse to clean it up for you.

No more bathing in my pons.
Keep your hair out of my sheath.
Stop partying in my ventricles
and tracking mud across my teeth.

My brain is just not big enough.
My temporal lobe is so tight it just might burst.
You may be dining in my memory
but, if I remember right, I was here first!

Scar

If
you think
I
can forget the
ice
of
your eye or the heat
of
your
thighs after midnight
then
you
have no idea how deep freezes
go
how
long fire lingers
or
how
far touch can reach,
no
idea
how sacred the finger prints
that
this
scar bears witness
to,
how
slowly and
reluctantly
the
skin
seeks
recovery
from
you.

Why I Love Mornings

Ah, the possibility
of the uncut tree
all the blank pages it holds
the unwritten words that
will carve their way
into branches
leaves
roots

The unopened gifts of morning
the untrammeled   untraveled
unimagined   unseen
unsounded   unmet
the ground still wet
or fresh with snow
something lost
or found.

I love the sunrise
for its seductive rays
inching themselves across
life's contours
inviting darkness out of corners
as night recedes
leaving the day smooth and untracked
like tide-soothed sands along the shore

I stand above the city
as the slow light
holds steadfast
a dull glow in the face of fog.
The sun is up
and day begins to settle
subtle and persevering
above the sparkling bay.

Below, the highway stretches
itself tight across the terrain.

The cars making their daily journeys
glisten with the possibility of changing
direction
taking the wrong exit
to the left or right
place.

How does one leave
without leaving behind?
How can I write the words
and let the tree stand?
Where does the dew go dry to
as the sun peels off the ordinariness of it all?
What will this day reveal?
What will the sun let fall?

IV. BELIEF

Seeing Is Not Believing

Conceptualism: *general ideas, such as the idea of house or happiness, not only exist explicitly in the human mind as concepts, but also implicitly in the minds of all people.*

she loves me. she loves me not. she loves me. she loves me not. she loves me. stripped of all, the daisy falls heavily to the floor.

Ascension

What must they have thought
God-fearing people
of surrounding towns
as James Sadler stoked his fire
and coaxed loose the ropes
that kept him in the meadow's hold?

More marvelous than Kitty Hawk
I suppose
was the miracle that rose
without wings
balancing on flames
above Christ Church green

careening with the wind
over cattle turned insignificant
looking beetle-sized on the horizon
as Mr. Sadler, rising like a sun,
discovered the overside of heaven
and destined himself for one of two skies:

The sky of Icarus
that taught the precariousness of altitude
the underside of flight
hurling a misguided boy to prideful death
at the moment he laughed victory
over height.

Or that silver sky
that stripped the cross of another son
and later gathered Mary up
to its cloudless breast.
The sky of mere ascension.
No return.

Aloft in a world of thatch and stone
Sadler rose above the heath
where gentle people tended flocks and mended fences.

What must they have thought
in Eighteenth-Century Oxfordshire
to see both gravity and god defied?

The scholars, perhaps, simply
toasted the science of it all.
They could see the lift off
could hear the roar of Sadler's flame
and knew how to gauge the mysteries
of math and physics.

While those walled outside
the academic garden
stood amid fields
among the bleating sheep growing small
as the silent something announced itself on the skyline.
Another error in Eden.

Today, a plaque hangs,
a footnote on the city wall:
James Sadler, First English Aeronaut
who in a fire balloon made a successful ascent
from near this place. On that forgotten date
to what unsure fate did witnesses turn?

Some may have shied away, trembling with fear
or run in search of shelter.
Some in their awe gently bowed.
Some, perhaps in wonder,
headed in full gallop toward the floating
inflated god.

Others still, lifted gaze
and sent prayers past
the great balloon.
Though no plaque was ever cast in bronze
to tell of the ascension,
they too rose.

Among Gargoyles

The fire-eyed hydra
the seven-headed serpent
the smiling demon
the sharp-tongued griffin
and the leering bird of prey.

The sharp-tongued griffin
one day and the goat-fish the next—
they salute me so singularly
that I'm certain
they are my next of kin.

That I'm certain
is no comfort, knowing
that when we lock eyes
it is I who turn
these medusas to stone.

It is I who turn
but the gargoyles themselves
haunt me like mirrors and howl down
in my own image
from every belfry and rooftop.

In my own image
is the world
of feather, scale, and bone.
Each fin and hoof
my own.

Each fin and hoof
around the corner
lurks like a concrete worm reflecting some snaky quality
in me
to be despised.

In me
and on the ancient ledge around the corner

I see myself hanging
looking over my distorted shoulder
not sure if I'm struggling to climb or fall.

Looking over my distorted shoulder
is a petrified Peryton
casting its dangerous shadow
at my feet while I keep trying
to bite my own tail.

At my feet while I keep trying
to look up, these gargoyles
mythic and massive
echo with every
pose: indignant, voracious, and appalling.

Echo with every
howl as I rage against the stone.
Only once did I turn a corner to find, perched like a painted virgin
on a frigate's prow,
a conspicuous bishop jutting out to bless me with granite fingers.

On a frigate's prow
the ocean can be familiar
and alien at once.
Even in this circus of stones
there are flowers.

Even in this circus of stones
grace blooms to remind me
that I too, perched as I am,
shall be the cornerstone
of some church.

The Idea of a Body

"Like a body wholly body"
—*Wallace Stevens*

curves shoulders thighs
like a body wholly body
loins tendons muscles
tits ass attitude
miss dee
miss can dee light
miss twilight at midnight
it's all right
alibi airtight
miss thing ain't missin'
a thing
a bawdy
wholly bawdy body
holy body
enshrined in hips
heels hair
spray
dis-
playing
this sacred
rite
of passage
like a body
wholly body
body
of literature
packed with meaning
body
of water
uncrossable
or miraculously parted
a body
wholly body
holy holy holy body

any body
every body
is some
body
wholly.

Wearing It Out

Go ahead, try it on.
Slip it over a shoulder.
Wrap it round your neck
when the weather blows colder.
Drop it down your back and around your chin.
Keep it loose. Let it flow. Tuck this poem in.

Don't be content with how it was made.
Adorn this poem in emeralds and jade.
Let this poem own the runway. Let it promenade.
Let it dazzle the pelvis and chill the eyes.
Embroider the cadence. Tint it with indigo dyes.
Wear this poem as you like. Accessorize!

Dress it up. Dress it down.
Wear it for comfort or fashion.
Wear it in. Wear it out.
Wear it with passion.
It's an all-weather poem, an all-purpose robe.
Dangle its lines from your very earlobes.

Ring your fingers with dactyls, iambs, and spondees.
Tattoo an anapest where only your lover will see.
Put loafers on these feet for some comic relief.
Bathe yourself luxuriously in this poem's leitmotif.
Let the meter bubble and the prosody foam.
Sharpen, then polish, the nails of this poem.

Gloss your lips till they drip
with its rhythms and rhymes.
Braid your hair into couplets.
Dress this poem to the nines.
Drape it, cape it, let it flutter behind.
Strap it, cap it, let it stutter and bind.

Cloak yourself in it. Clutch it in like a purse.
Wear it forward or sideways or in reverse.
Wear this poem like armor—solid and steel.

Carry the words like swords, if that's how you feel.
Lace it up tightly from your ankles to knees.
Go on, wear this poem tightly, or however you please.

Don't be afraid of the other extreme.
Wear this poem strapless, crotchless
or split down the seam.
This poem has potential, so much appeal.
Wear it as an underpoem.
Let it reveal.

Let it jangle and bangle.
Striped and star-spangled.
Or, if you prefer, dress down
to its barest of bones.
Go ahead, pierce your nose
with this poem.

Put holes in its knees. Tatter its cuffs.
Let it fade. Let it tear.
Treat it real rough.
Then hand it on down when you've had enough.
Let it dance in new shoes. Feel free to share.
Pass this poem on for others to wear.

Any Shell

Every periwinkle
knows it.
Each nautilus
and conch will tell you.
Even the most common
scallop
understands
that cell phones
at the beach
are an insult
to the whole ocean
a slap in the face
of the entire sea.

Death Sings

Death sings
in the echo
of things unsaid
and swims
in oceans filled
with the failure
of words.
To understand how language fails
try spelling the siren's wail
the screech of tires
the moment of impact
the gasp of the crowd.

The first domino falls
one rectangular dotted blow
causing the next.
Death falls
in the woods.
A faulty watch.
Poor navigation.
Asleep
at the wheel.
Nobody hears.

But I have
heard it.
Even in public places.
In celebrations and spontaneous elation
like the crack of a bat:
Pow!
Ball game over.
The defeated pitcher moves
one loss closer
to his last fast ball.
So much for the save.
The triumphant batter
having so narrowly
escaped rebuff

reaches up and out
pressing palms with joyful teammates:

high fives
the modern victory prayer
players share in a moment's jubilation.

All
        as Death sings   *Take me out to the ball game...*
an offering   *Buy me some peanuts and cracker jacks*
        one win closer   *I don't care if I ever come back*
a standing ovation   *So it's root, root, root for the home team*
        one loss closer   *If they don't win*
                              it's a shame
and consolation   *So it's one, two, three strikes you're out*
        to each.   *at the ol' ball game*

Buying Time

There's a sale on minutes this week
but I'm in need of bigger units.
Perhaps a month
in the country
a year in Provence
a walk in the sunshine.

A few extra moments
of mindfulness
won't last me
through the fortnight.

What are they charging
for decades these days?

I would need at least a century
to follow your scent
an even longer stint to catch your train
of thought
but only a twinkling
was needed
to know
where I want to spend my always.

There is a sale on minutes
this week
but I'm not bargain hunting right now.

I will pay full fare
for a dozen Octobers today.
I love the turn of the leaves
the sharp smell of harvest
and the long stretch of twilight.
Besides, I want to celebrate
your birthday often
at least
once a month.

How

I love you
circularly
squarely
linearly
and non-linearly
I love you
solid
liquid
formless
shapeless
I love you
in a sequence
with patterns
erratically
chaotically
between parameters
and beyond
I love you
endlessly
ceaselessly
irregularly
I love you
with
and
or without
structure
I love you love you love you
you I love
love you
I do
love you
I do
I do
I do
love
I do
love
you

My Mother's Tulips

My mother's tulips are made of wood,
her birds too.
Acrylic rainbows stretch across a stained-glass sky
while crescent moons orbit and crystal saturns turn
in delightful patterns
around the sunlit rooms.

The palm fronds and grasses grow
high in my mother's den.
Eagles, balloons, fairy dragons and baboons
soar across the airy loft
while polished puffins by the score
stand sentry at the door.

What a galaxy
of strange imagination
my mother's house
has grown to be—
a Big Bang of free association, everywhere creation!
No species is endangered there.

Dinosaurs and dodos
Dorothy and Toto
werewolves to howl with
hippos and hydras to climb on
a horseless saddle to ride
to wherever you want to go.

And that's only inside.
Outside, a lady slipper trail
surrounds a leafy yard
where standing gruff guard
is a pair of stony-frown goblins
looking down on a stone deaf mutt named Duffy.

My father seems at home there
slightly amused
by Mom's menagerie.

But he is no idle onlooker.
As much a keeper of this zoo
as she is he.

My mother's tulips are made of wood.
Her birds too.
She crafts, collects
and takes orphans in.
I wonder sometimes
if I might have been

discovered on a roadside stop
picked from a yard sale or a county swap.
Or my mother,
having seen something
in *Better Homes and Gardens*,
carved me at midnight in her cluttered workshop.

Sometimes
when the starlight falls just right
upon the fireplace
a smoky shadow of a girl
whose face might look like mine
hides amid the sparks behind the fire screen.

It seems to me
that like Geppetto before them
my parents
bring things still
and silent
to life.

The tulips may be made of wood,
the birds too.
But for those listening with gem-filled ears
the chirps, the twitters, the sing-songs are there to hear.
For those who breathe imagination
the petal fragrances are strong.

Enchantment abides in my mother's mild garden.
A thousand deep-spun charms and wild spells

are cast by every ray of sunshine, each drop of pollen.
Sorcery rains on this corner of the suburb.
The trees stand full of goodness, undisturbed.
The fruit hangs succulent, tempting and still unfallen.

V. KNOWLEDGE

Knowledge

Dialectical Materialism: *matter is the primary reality.*

teeth. muscle. hair. tendons. skin. *Children sometimes go with each other to the closet.* movement. *and often their talk is not.* friction. *what it should be.* fluctuation. *The little girl who values her modesty.* flow. *who thinks highly of herself.* solid. *will never allow anyone to talk to her.* inertia. *concerning any part of her body.* mass. *in a way that is not sweet and pure.* liquid. *and if any child ventures to give her information concerning herself.* substance. *that seems to her such as she would not tell her mother.* presence. *the wisest thing for her.* progress. *to do.* matter. *would be to say: I would rather.* lightness. *you would not.* force. *tell me about it.*

Italicized passage from *What A Girl Ought To Know*, by Mrs. Mary Wood-Allen, M.D., National Superintendent of the Purity Department Women's Christian Temperance Union, published as part of the Self and Sex Series by The Vir Publishing Company, Philadelphia, PA, 1897, p. 110.

What Keeps You Awake

2:33 a.m.
it's my turn to cross
my fingers
make a wish

no one here to uncross them

I swear by the three ones
on the brim of your hat
that our wishes
overlap

now is the hour you roam

carving words into your forearm
whispering to the ivy
embracing your corner of the night
deciding which pages to unwrite

as if to inscribe silence will erase the truth

words can validate
disbelief
fulfill your wish
for relief

but reality burns even when there are no pages to destroy

words never
written
can do damage
too

traffic fades but not despair

in this city
lovely enough
to make bones curl

and time crawl

the sleepless fog seeps into every memory

did this same thick sheet of air
linger there
where you are
gathering moisture from your tears

before arriving here?

did this misty shroud
cloud your vision
and admire the knives
with you?

did it leave you cold?

what keeps you warm
what keeps you awake
what keeps you
what keeps

you dislike the word: "examined"

the unexamined life
is not worth
living.
That's Plato

but "expunge" is one word you can live with
believe it or not
things never lost have
been found

so much remains unexamined

or at least
unsaid
and though you speak them
they are not your words

"exaggerating"

 "I'm exaggerating"
"that I'm exaggerating"
"say that I'm exaggerating"
"he'll say that I'm exaggerating"

you betray yourself by letting his measure do your math

you relentlessly chew and then swallow your crushed pride
allowing him to tell you
the long
and short of it all

his lies do not account for facts

you've tuned your radio to his official story
set your clocks to someone else's time
gauged your bearings with his compass
unguided even by your own sky

the sky that has burned your shadow into the hillside

you are out there somewhere
and I'm inside digging
through the attic
of my own forgotten words

hoping a few will let me hang my hat on them

words so old
that they may have dried out
and flaked off the only pages
that ever held them

words I wrote to myself, a foothold, something to point me in
      the right direction

then out of a dog-eared journal they crawl
as if on command, as if it were yesterday that hope was born
words I burned into an empty long ago page

to light my own hollow cell:

don't throw a rope
just send the map
that helps me find the road from here
to myself

If madness were a
virtue and silence a crime
I could be myself.

What Matters

Long before Hydrogen
and Oxygen had names
Water was believed the common matter
from which all else was made.

Then with an eye turned towards the sky
a new truth was declared
and Air was known to be
the element that earthly substance shared.

So on and on the theories marched
as theorists lived and died.
From alchemy to DNA,
new equations were devised

Till in this age of splitting atoms
virtual this and virtual that
it's easy to imagine
birth in test tubes and puberty in vats

but there you stand
outside the science of it all
you butt naked and alive
wet, airy, boundless

and unknown
you stand beyond conjecture
transcending hypothesis
and way past stone

hydrogen
oxygen
toenails
teeth and drool

you stand there breathing blinking balancing
you stand there dripping—
in what primordial pool

have you been skinny dipping?

wet with the four directions
light with Heaven's weight
of the star-eyed Seven Sisters
you are number eight

your whispers stir creation
your cough can spill the sky
galaxies have imploded
on the pinhead of your single sigh

amid miracle and mystery
scientists extrapolate
building towers of ice-dry theory
while lovers, too, exaggerate

how dear of me to say
you mean the world to me
how queer of me to praise
the elemental life force with your name

but then you lift your lids
to reveal the great beyond
and in one moment's blink
another aeon gone

Without a Compass

Skating over your shins
traversing each calf
reaching the height of your thighs

cresting each breast
with all the deliberateness
of topping Everest

climbing the slope
of your nose
with my tongue

crashing through
the grassy plains
of your lashes

at last I find myself
lost in the forest of your hair
with no wish to find my way back to anywhere but you.

Scaling your cheekbones
I pause to catch my breath
on your upper lip.

Upon discovering the cave
of your mouth
I enter

hoping that you will let me
call all of you
home.

Here Are Hills

Here are hills
unlike others

Hills to be
mounted
burrowed
tilled
hidden
borrowed
treasured
planted
filled

Mountains
to be moved

Roll yourself silly
down these sides
take a spill
slide
glide
stride
once
twice
when
it feels right

Invite these slopes
to change
direction
to face the sun
to take a challenge
give a thrill
once
twice
whatever feels right

Here are hills
unlike others

Climb on

I Imagine Them

turning some dog-eared page
tapping out a drum beat on the dash
sorting the laundry
digging for a matching sock
buried in deep pockets
breaking an egg on the side of a bowl
fingering guitar strings

Where are they now?

tenderly holding a pen to paper
furiously moving though air
in concert
with your conversation
resting assuredly on the back
of a chair

oh to be the steering wheel
or the spoon
to have your palms
pressed solidly upon me
the full fan of your fingers
curved to the slope
of my shoulders
oh to be warmed
to be wrapped
in hope
to be healed
by the laying on
of your hands

Harvest

Do not let a woman with a sexy rump deceive you
with wheedling and coaxing words; she is after your barn.

—Hesiod

Shall we gather the sunset
pluck what is ripe
harness the cicada's song?
Even if this isn't the season
of new love
let us remember the buds
and reap what we can.
No crop is too small.
No harvest too lean.
The grain will yield.
So scatter and slash
call in the cows
and let us milk them all dry.
Plow as you will.
Bulldoze away.
Why not make every season
our season
each day
our day
to till and tease
to clear and seed
to plant and replant
as we please.
Come
my sweet smell of hay
do not be deceived
by Hesiod.
He says that I am
after your barn.
I want the whole
fucking farm!

Sapphic Chords

On what marble stones would you scratch your love today?
Spray it on brick walls, rap it in pool halls,
hang it on the clothes line with your lingerie?
Oh, Sappho!

Would you swing a softball bat, wear lipstick, ride a Harley?
What novels would you pen, what political party?
Is that really tenderness in your final line, or do words hang for what you
couldn't say?

What remnants you left behind, too little but enough
for us to know the luxury of your lust.
Your heat, your wisdom, your passion—all left in fragmented trust.
Oh, Sappho!

On the Eighth Day Adam Slept Alone

It must have been
the eighth day.

A day the scribes and Pharisees conveniently
left out.

Adam was either inspecting goats
or naming the birds

when something pinched
my side.

I had to stop pruning the tree of knowledge
to catch my breath.

God had taken a long weekend.

At first I thought the solitude of gardening
was going to my head.

Was it loneliness?
An omen? A vision?

For a moment I thought I would
ascend.

Then I realized it was just a rib
missing.

How you found your way in
along the banks of the third river

I will never know
but I still shiver to recall

how perfectly your fingers
fell into place

along the ridges
of my ribcage.

Go ahead, Love,
take every last bone.

Make of me
what you will.

VI. EVOLUTION

Evolving

Naturalism: *all reality can be accounted for through the physical and the human sciences.*

attraction. her eyes blue and quick. acceleration. reflex. inertia. touch. tremble. drawn to her like shallow light in the afternoon. impulses. momentum. seasons. her knees cupped in my palms. adhesion. growth. thirst. numb. learn to live with fog. adaptation. growth. soothed over by the deep hum. her hands spilling as she speaks of tidepools. one if by chill. two if by thaw. mineral slowly replacing organic. say it. still stone. say it again. alone. petrified. evolve or...

Stirred Awake

Every morning
I am stirred
sometimes at 4 AM
sometimes at 5 or 5:30
and I am sure
that it is you
waking
me
it is you rising
from your side
of the bed
on your side
of the continent.

Wildflowers

Just as the dinosaurs
were running on their last
collective soon-to-be extinct leg
the wildflowers took hold—
blooming, seeding, spreading
themselves thinly and thoroughly.
Landscape scraped rough by jagged cliffs of ice
yielded to the supple shoots of tap roots
and permitted fibrous tendrils to
weave themselves through turf
once trod upon by Tyrannosaurus Rex.

In the spring of that ancient age
liverwort, fleabane, and coltsfoot
announced the next generation.
Against all odds,
with leaves toothed and lobed,
petals lipped and winged,
and surely with humility,
tiny buds unfolded
their colorful palettes
and set up their fragrant shop.

Bladderwort and sundew
played evolutionary tricks
on passing gnats
while cockleburs and beggar's ticks
let tiny spores spread the gift
of their good news.
Sea thrift, beach pea, and swamp rose mallow
padded shallow shorelines
not far from where the last of the kronosaurs
swam her final ocean mile.

In wetlands
where stegosaurus tracks
had faded from the swampy floor
spatterdock and pickerelweed

shrouded giant reptile graves
in purple, yellow, green leafy haze.
Hunters and gatherers alike
found themselves prey
to weather systems
as the Paleozoic gave way to
heliotropic: the one constant
in a changing world, the sun, held final sway.

Out with triceratops and mastodons.
In with the quiet bloodroot
and prophetic forget-me-not.
A soft and supple society
of jewelweed and heartsease
rose where the big-boned empire fell.

And I, like the simplest day lily
obedient to the sun's rays,
find myself turned
your way
locked in a circadian whirl
and hopeful that the unnoticed
wildflower of my love
translucent and vulnerable as it is
will prove strong enough
to take gentle hold
in your wilderness
for a while.

Natural History

Bones without marrow
rib-caged and narrow
stand in postures
of permanence.

Bleached and unblooded
this peaceful parade of prehistory
outmarches the very extinctions
left sadly behind.

It's hard to tell the spires
from the spines
the arches from the
archeology

In the natural
history museum
imagination gels
with fabrication

Sunlight pours in
at all angles
and tangles with the
tibia and fibula of time.

Are we inside
the whale
or outside looking
inward?

The jaws the claws
the wingspan of the afterhour
draws us toward the rafters
amid the shadows

Inspiring
conspiring belief
in a higher power

(dare I say god?)

The gathering storm
of the future
rises
like a pterodactyl

Asking the password
and my answer
falls
flat on its own bone.

What creatures
with features unknown
stand ready to pass
or let me in on their secrets?

Carved into walls
stony serpents, water-spout wolves
and a lion with a sage's head
bear witness to the designs of other ages.

Architects
real and imagined
have stamped this world
with buttresses buttonholes and billionaires.

Little matters now
to the Dodo Bird
fed fat by keepers who failed
to preserve the last of her flightless line.

Tell me in a word—What is beauty?
Where is art? Is all life plunder?
Why not start again, this time with a fist
full of wonder and thaw?

After the thunder and relentless rain
when the dove finds no olive branch, no dry perch,
shall we meet again, shall we bubble and lurch
in the giant primordial puddle?

Outside a single raven seeks
in this place
a haven
hopping afoot in search of string and straw.

In the museum
past and present build a nest
while the future
knocks at the door.

Under this circus tent of bone, brick and cement,
in the belly of this stranded whale,
who cannot hear the thin cry
of Jonah's heavy lament?

Continental Drift

you have moved through
like an ice flow—
steady slow substantial

tumble of glacial tongue
sweeping through
valleys reshaped

you arrived on your own epic time
patient and thorough
meltwater firn crevasse and all

lifting rock on shifting plates
smoothing edges
and moving the very axis of my teeth

you soothed over rifts and fault lines
leaving me
newly minted

peaked and ridged
steep and crested
sloped and spurred

Hillsides lush
and summits glistening
I rush to a new dawn

but not without raw traces
of your tender era
scratched warmly on my every acre

No Butterfly Hears

If the single stroke
of a butterfly wing
can fan the forces
gathering on a peaceful ocean
and set the blue tsunami
into motion,
then who is to say
that the flames of genocide
have not been stoked
by the wide ripple of a Grizzled Skipper
lightly dancing upon a far off field?

Or that a mudslide just outside
Mexico City could not be traced
to a Mountain Ringlet's change in direction?
Or that one parent's anger
hurled against a child's cheek
has not been fueled by the rustle
of this White-Letter Hairstreak?

These delicate flying carpets
that sliver and dart
above quivering blades
of grass
take little notice
of the world beyond
lift off / hover / alight / feed / lift off again.

Miles and years beyond
one Grayling's gentle gyrations
a giant redwood crashes to the floor
and no butterfly
hears.

The swoop of a Red Admiral
wakes a roaring hunger
while the hover of a Silver-Washed Fritillary
soothes maternal fear

and the subtle misstep
of a Mazarine Blue
ushers in the next
ice age

And here just inches above
the frantic flutter
of a Camberwell Beauty
my heart skips
a wing beat
of its own
because   on the other side of the globe   you have thought yourself unloved.

The Drain of Winter

The drain of winter weights this sparrow's wing.
She sees the world through stiff and frozen eye.
An offshore stir will turn her loose to spring.

A storm around her has been gathering,
The turbulence of having known "good-bye."
The drain of winter weights this sparrow's wing.

Where flew the rhymes she used to sing?
Where fled the drafts she rode across the sky?
What offshore stir will turn her loose to spring?

Wrapped in foggy frosty whisperings.
Trapped in ice without the will to fly.
The drain of winter weights this sparrow's wing.

Then mild and gentle comes an offering.
A feather kindness softly brushes by.
An offshore stir, turning her loose to spring.

I've dreamt about the thaw your breath will bring,
So gust and gale until your lungs run dry.
The drain of winter leaves the sparrow's wing.
An offshore stir has turned us loose to spring.

Greenery

Juniper, Oracle Oak and Hop Tree,
California Buckeye, and Elderberry.
Pacific Dogwood and the pale green Eucalyptus,
Quaking Aspen and Flannelbush.

raw, sprouting, lush
green love
green with envy
green with youth
green with early spring

olive, emerald, avocado,
greenlight
ready, set, GO!
greenhouse, greenbelts, ocean kelp,
cucumber, lizard, lime and forest green,
spruce, teal, and putting green.

green-eyed, verdant, grassy, immature
green and leafy
green half-formed
tender, pleasant, alluring
temperate
freshly sawed
vigorous
not ripe
yet
promising

greenbriar, greenbug, green dragon
greenshanks running along the ocean's edge
greenlings swimming
greenlets singing
greengage plums
green thumbs
greenhorns
and greenflies—
how on earth

amid sage swells
kelly hillsides
and swirls of firs
did I ever find
that green of
hers?

holly, drake, and brewster green,
pistachio, shamrock, serpentine
terre verde, Brunswick, tourmaline,
lotus, jade, and spinach green:
start to finish
lowlands to highs
no field, no forest, no leaf, no blade
can catch the light or trap the shade;
no earthly tones will ever rise
to match the green
enchantment
of her eyes.

The Poet Explains the Symmetry of
the Universe to the Physicist

Wishful
      is the symmetry
            the physicist craves.

Time and space
of the minuscule
           in conspicuous conflict with
                  the godless face
                  of the galaxies.

The clash of Einstein's quantum equations   with the minuscule gospel of quarks.

Forget the spectral lines
the hadron strings
and other hypothetical bonds.
Let me tell you about physics.
Let me add it all up,
multiply the warp
and the woof
of it all.
Let me reveal the symmetry.

Leave me to peel back
the ends
and unwrap
this time-space fabric
that traps us all
the bends
and blows
of emotion
are my laboratory
as I uncoil
the tangles
our everyday
experiments weave.

Leave me to
chart
the momentum
and decay

what is left
visible
in the wake
of the passions

forces
as unmeasurable
as they are
tangible

like love
and
jealousy
the keys

to entering
the six
unfathomable
directions.

Sure
the theory
can be
beautiful
prophetic too:
        the eight-fold way predicting new particles,
            black holes locking protons into stellar lives
            no more our own invention than
            the Archer, the Lion, the Twins, the Scales, the Water Bearer ...

equationlessness can be proof too

                Like the poor hypothetical cat
                trapped in someone's
                thought box
                with imagined flask

shattered

the cat
suspended in two states of being
at one time:
in need of both milk
and burial.

just conjure up an elliptical score
written in stars
dictating the cosmos into
being
dream the microscopic violas
and violins
superstrings
vibrating it all into existence.

But let theory
like poetry
emerge
from
emotion
in practice
revealing precisely
the knowledge that scientists lack
what their wish for consistency conceals:
the real symmetry rests not between the largest and smallest infinities
but between one contradiction
and the other.

Emotions as evidence
that rules
of the minuscule
unravel
when one travels
to the outer
galaxies.
Let passion
teach science
that if we begin to believe
in the theories
we spin

then
the laws
the religions—
all
soon falls
away
as we move
from the mega to the micro
from the general
to the specific
from nations
from tribes
to our families
to our lovers
to ourselves
time and space lose
their seamlessness
all bends
time warps
space collapses
gravity may
or may not
hold
relativity is
no more
real
or less real
than the zodiac wheel
than the constellations
than the prophets
who read them
no more
real
or less real
than the stars
than the sky
than our own
insignificant
miraculous
lives.

All Is Becoming

How they balance the scales
fine-tune the micrometer
calibrate the barometer
I will never know.

Still, scientists claim
to measure
disorder.
"Entropy"

they call it
equate it with inertia
and from it predict
demise

the inevitable unraveling
the random reactions
all roads leading to
break down

or break up
Kosovo
Rwanda
the fall of Rome.

Shall we embrace
this race
against
everything?

Do we dare to bow
to entropy
or to resist its blows?
How can one hold

the ungraspable
jumble
of life

clamoring for stability

amid change
demanding movement
in spite of stillness
folding joy into turmoil

blending you
with me
saying stay
and go
wanting together
and apart?

Solitude may be
an escape
from upheaval
but
confusion
is growth
in the uproar
that is this eight-star stir.
I love my bedlam.
I would never ask for more
or less
of the turbulence
that is you
the pandemonium
that is me
the commotion
that is us
confused crude and alive
muddled and spinning
on this unfixed axis
I am a breathing
experiment
in thermotaxis
bound to move
toward
        or away from
heat

then just as
all is becoming
something
else
        from the chaos
                    you emerge
                            whole
                                aflame
                                and exquisite.
                                        And for this
                                        the scientists
                                        have no name.
                                    For this all measurement fails.
                    Apostles rush to gather scrolls to record your arrival.
                                Mythologists frame their legends.
                                            Bards drool.
                                    The very breath of you
                                    becomes the air of lore.
                                    Yes, you are the miracle
                                        worth writing for.

VII. TENSION

The Anxious Seat at the Table

Existentialism: *absence of any universal values in which a state of anxiety, known as angst, characterizes the human condition as a result of the dread that arises from being totally responsible for all of one's choices.*

oyster fork. dessert fork. salad fork. which one? fish. dinner. fondue. hay fork. this one? carving fork. cocktail fork. south fork. fork it over. forklift. spoon. pitch fork. forked tongue. fingers forked. fork in the road.

Foothold

My stride today
is twice the length
it was then
but still I feel small
enough to crawl
under fallen leaves.

The landscape
remains
almost unchanged:
moss along the embankment
more but smaller birds, taller reeds,
and trees arching above the familiar weave of trail.

This path around the swamp
is home
to my desert crossings
frontier battles
pirate mutinies
and arctic expeditions.

No signs of recent adventurers
but I am sure
that this murky water still teems
with wetland spirits who slither
and slog though the underworld
of this mysterious bog.

I know the curve
of every bare-bark root
the length to which
each branch can hold my weight
and the location of
a hundred secret hide-aways:

The oak that broke my arm
the cove where we practiced
taxidermy on roadkill

the sandpit where we smoked
unfiltered Kents pilfered
from someone's mother's pocketbook.

The sagging patch of skunk cabbage
looks withered but the stink
remains strong. I can't help
picking up an acorn to hurl
at the pine we used to pebble
with slingshot fire.

If I climb the embankment
the swamp will run dry
in the rush of new homes new cars new neighbors.
Just over the rise
lies a street lined with the present and strangers
who threaten to ambush my memory.

So I stay low, along the water's edge,
comforted to find that the path around the swamp
still holds
the child
I sometimes lose
track of.

Prayer Meeting

In memory of Randy Shilts and Matthew Shepard

What prince of peace
what beacon
what pillar
of salt
in our wounds
is this
arriving with his platoon
of frenzied followers?

Our Father

At the pearly
airport gate
with no baggage to claim
but holy hate
and twisted Bible verses
well rehearsed
but not so well
interpreted.

I pledge allegiance to the flag

Time to spew
to anyone who will
put him on TV
he fires off a round
of born-again babble
leading his flock
down-
town.

Of the United States of America

Already late
for the start of the service

the misguided march to the church
armed with their certainty
spray-painted on poster board,
a trinity of words
for the funeral:
GOD HATES FAGS

Who art in Heaven

What is there
to protest
in a death?
What is there
to say
if you believe
God's will is done
on earth as it is in heaven?

Hallowed be Thy name

Inside the churches
the bands play
on
and celebrate
lives
ended early
by a virus
or a beating.

And to the Republic

Outside
the man who believes
himself to be called
is so busy listening
to his own voice declare
God's will
that he fails to hear the voices inside
giving new life to the fallen ones.

For which it stands

So the man
who thinks he knows
God's will
who lets himself be called
Reverend
leads his pale lemmings
to the ledge
of darkness

Thy kingdom come

while those he would
have burn
walk together
in the life
tongues ablaze
united
with love
and rage.

Thy will be done

So blind is the man
armed with magic markers
and cardboard
that he misses the miracle before him.

On earth

The spirits of the ones
to be buried
are lifted above us all
on the breath of a loving multitude

One nation

far more potent
than a virus
more righteous
than a raised fist

under God

more enduring than
the flesh.

Indivisible

The patchwork assembly
share a song so strong
that its chorus echoes
after and before us

With liberty and justice for all

beyond imagination and
well into any
Armageddon
that might dare to arrive

On earth as it is in heaven

Night Fishing in Gifu

The torches burn bright on the Nagara.
　　Night shivers
　　　　across the water
　　　　　　as the flames ride

through the distant dark,
　　　　their lights letting everyone know
　　　　　　that the fishing boats
　　　　　　　　are about to arrive.

Anticipation ripples
　　　　through the crowd gathered
　　　　　　for a night
　　　　　　　　of Ukai.

The river laps against the shore.
　　　　The fleet appears.
　　　　　　In each boat a man
　　　　　　　　ready in his ancient art

in hand a dozen ropes
　　　　leading to a dozen
　　　　　　hopeful throats
　　　　　　　　of a dozen hungry birds.

I know how the cormorants feel.
　　　　Slender creatures unfed
　　　　　　since the last
　　　　　　　　yesterday.

Hunger sharp
　　　　eyes alert
　　　　　　the birds are sent for food
　　　　　　　　they cannot eat.

They flap and dive
　　　　obedient and skilled
　　　　　　gathering up ayu
　　　　　　　　in their long bills.

Fish tails spill
    from corners
        of bird mouths.
           At best,

a meager drop
    of finned and scaly flavor
        runs a tease
           over taste buds.

Irises are full bloom in Gifu
    but this feeding time
        only an illusion
           for the birds.

Night in and out
    strings tighten
        around long elegant throats
           to prevent them

from swallowing
    what they catch
        to forbid them
           from having their fill.

In spite of longing
    the hungry continue on
        fetching what they cannot
        have.

Unaware of the eki-sha
    who reads
        unspeakable fortunes
        with thin sticks,

the hungry
    complete their task
        turning the unkeepable catch
           back to the greedy baskets

back for others
　　　　to feast upon
　　　　　　back to
　　　　　　　　the ravenous night.

Uninvited at this dance
　　　　of hungry birds
　　　　　　we are wallflowers
　　　　　　　　hanging on this shore.

The grace with which the cormorants
　　　　move through the water
　　　　　　and through the open sky
　　　　　　　　still overwhelms the watcher.

Leashed birds
　　　　darting
　　　　　　between stars
　　　　　　　　at the hour of the ox

so much of me
　　　　rocked
　　　　　　by the pull
　　　　　　　　of almost

the near unbearability
　　　　of so close
　　　　　　the beauty of taste
　　　　　　　　without touch.

Of Underdogs and If Onlys

In memory of Glenn Burke

It seemed to me that everyone else
backed champion after invincible champion
teams with legitimate dynasties
athletes who rewrote record books
horses that triumphed down the stretch.
My brother could root for a team
as far away as Green Bay
as long as crew-cut linemen
shouldered Lombardi to victory
upon sweet victory.

I don't recall ever backing a winner.
I placed my bets elsewhere
on the Almosts of the world
unheralded names like Curt Flood,
the cutest quarterback, Roman Gabriel,
and the shortest Celtic, Artie Williams.
Something in a bio or a smile
could win me over—
a willingness to take a stand
take the heat
or endure obscurity.
I worshipped those who gave
beyond the boundaries of their sport.
Haunted by the drama of
What Could Have Been
I pulled for the
Underdogs and If Onlys
who lost their way
in the jungle
of their own potential
or found themselves caught
in the snare of lies
about what it takes
to reach the top.

I took it personally
when a contender
fell shy or short
or stumbled on a snare
of expectations.
My throat tightened
and my head spun
when heroes choked away
a contest they
"should have" won.

I still choose unlikely heroes.
I listen for the rumors
and read between the lines
how the football hero cooks for friends
the goalie has no time for "romance"
the rookie is married to the game
and the golfer reads *Tales of the City* between rounds.

I figure there are handicaps
reporters never mention.
What fear of the word "faggot"
does to a batting average,
how one's T-cell count factors in
to the difficulty of a triple gainer.
Does your jump shot suffer
when you are surrounded by men
who abuse the women in their lives
while claiming to be Born Again
then refuse to look you in the eye
because you have no woman
in your life
to terrorize?

To survive at all
in some circumstances
is a miracle.
To exist in spite of enemies
is victory.

Numbing the pain
may not make you
a hero
but when every winded breath
you breathe
is an invisible blast
of resistance
then you too deserve
to be cheered
while still alive
and one day
chaired
through the marketplace.

And you, Glenn, were well-named a Dodger.
You ducked the expectations
avoided the prying lenses
slipped through the narrow cracks
on your way to the majors.
I can only imagine how heartbreak
and betrayal
eroded your talented marrow.
Each mannish embrace
a silent slap in the face
because a too-intimate touch
might reveal too much.
Rumors about your life
a contract bonus for landing a wife
everyone wanting something
and you just wanting to find
your rhythm at the plate
never trusting the words "I love you"
until too late.

                    Coaches, teammates, lovers, even drugs,
                    let you down
                    hard.

How does anyone remain whole when
What Might Have Been was stolen
so long ago without as much
as an admission that the thief

was the game
you loved?

Baseball has not
as they say
been very good to you.

How could it feel like anyone
was pulling
for you
with so much pulling
at you?

How could you ever be more
than a shadow of
the talent you
possessed?

Yet you celebrated the game
with jubilation and whimsy
dancing with Dusty
as you two clapped the first high-five
into existence.
You reached out to teammates
even when they would not reach back.
It's not
then
surprising that you finally fell.

What makes yours a life and a career
of epic proportion
is that you strove as doggedly
fought as bravely
and rose as
gallantly
as you did.

What you might have been, Glenn,
is not nearly as important
as who you really were.

Sublimation

"Do you see how sublimation is almost the opposite of repression?"

Pulling my chin
to the bar
I imagine
her lips

I sit
in this chair
because I cannot climb
into her lap

Running along
the beach
I sprint
because I cannot chase her, catch her, extend my reach

When I write
every finger finds
its way through the maze of keys
fiery strokes meant for her hair

The newspaper offers something to think about
when I cannot scan
the breadth and depth of
her eyes

I wash the car
touching even the bumper with grace
because I cannot rub along her lovely thighs
I must not caress that beautiful face

Unexpressed meaning harbored
in every bite
stowed away in every breath
held captive by her light.

Even the water I drink
knows that each swallow
is a rewriting
of instinct.

What do I care of
Freud? Of the Ego's dance
with the Id? How easy it is
to understand the psychology of it all

When every act
no matter how small
or mundane
reigns in a wild craving.

But the chemistry
is far less
easy
to explain

How one
restrains
so much
how one defies the impulse.

Does one choose to interrupt
the fogging of the mirror?
Could I put an end to condensation?
How can the poet dare not eat that peach?

The chemistry
remains
beyond explanation

Just when I think
that the spine of me
is going liquid

at the moment I imagine
that I am going to melt

I feel myself rising
uplifted

transformed
I feel the gentle gift of elevation

then
when I least
expect it

still
rising
my body shifts
from solid
to air

Perhaps it is all conscious
a choosing
a sublimation of urge
a reshaping of desire

but as my body
slides
from solid to air
(leap-frogging entirely
its liquid state)
I am well aware
that it is not
all
in the mind.

Stolen Flames

Had'st thou broached
Thy little Plan to Die

—*Emily Dickinson*

In olden days
bold women
went quickly.
Gravity
and a sharp blade
made Marie Antoinette's head fall.
Joan of Arc just went up
in flames.
Antigone chose to hang bravely
from a silky slipknot
robbing Creon of his little plan:
her slow death
by starvation
in a sealed cave.

Our evolution has been a slow
disturbing one.
We women have adapted well
keeping hearts abeat
blood aflow
and our breathing steady
as our reasoning dissolved.
Our brains became
vestigial organs
as we shelved logic
and lost resolve
to save ourselves.

The venomous asp
gave Cleopatra
the speedy exit
that she craved.
And Virginia Woolf

piled her pockets
with a stony guarantee
that she become one
with the unbiased waves.

Women used to know
how to be decisive.

We have become
alien step-daughters to
our own mothers
having learned to
to dull the knife
to slow the pulse
to keep the body alive
to walk on earth
a half-step ahead of death.

The Year of the Woman.
Hang her
on a billboard.
Slap her
on the side of a bus.
Let her string herself up
in a bikini
ravished and unraveling
wafer thin and frail
needle marks not suggestive
of needlepoint
nailed into unseen veins
eyes vacant like the empty hours
of waiting to be noticed
the biggest fear
the size of
thighs
the only meal
a fully digested lie
that who we are
is something separate
from how we look
or how available

or how desperate.

We let ourselves die slowly
stretching death to fit the life span
in silent compliance
to a most unnatural
selection.

The witch hunts never ended.
We have just invited them in
to our own
heads.
Prosecutors and jurors
at our own trials—
self-charged
self-convicted
and repeatedly
self-sentenced
to longing and
self-loathing.

It is easy to cooperate
to make a little plan
or just to let death be
life's constant escort.
No need to tie us to the stake
no cause for rocks
in our pockets
when we are so willing
to take our batterings again
and again.

A girl once named Cassandra
asks across a timeless ocean
long after her own matted ashes
have been scattered
by ancient
blasts:
At what stakes
will you women
burn?

On modern beaches
fragile girls line the sand
and lather their waifish selves
in oils
before turning
unlistening ears
to the stiff wind.
The sun beats down.
A stone rolls across
the mouth
of the cave
a living
grave
of our own
digging.

The Newspaper Made No Connection:
a mostly found poem, July 1995

Rejecting the hero status bestowed on Pete Wilson by Aryan Nation, the governor's office insisted Saturday that his successful assault on affirmative action has been "misunderstood" by white supremacists.

—*S.F. Examiner*

HAYDEN LAKE, Idaho—
Beneath tall, whispering
pines and a large
swastika banner
hanging
from a church tower, white
supremacists
from around the country and
Canada
gathered here
this weekend
for the Aryan World Congress,
an annual celebration
of the white race
and anti-Semitism....

SAN FRANCISCO, California—
University of California Regents
gathered to dismantle the
Affirmative Action practices
established to address
exclusionary processes

The New Tribalism
exclusionary
exclusionary processes
To address exclusionary processes
Practices established to address exclusionary processes
To dismantle the practices established to address exclusionary processes
Gathered to dismantle the practices established to address exclusionary processes
University of California Regents

...Amid *Sieg Heil* salutes
and with Nazi symbols
festooning their clothes,
participants paid $45 each to enter the gates
of The Church of Jesus Christ Christian Aryan Nations
for two days of speeches and ceremonies,
highlighted by Saturday night's
solemn
cross-burning
service ... .

Don't let your sons or daughters
pass through the gates
of any church
that feels the need
to bless Jesus
with more than one modifier.
What do these particular church-goers do
on the remaining 363 days a year
when speeches and cross-burnings
are not enough?

The Church of Jesus Christ Christian Aryan Nations

What are the church members who cannot afford
the forty-five dollar cover charge
up to this evening?

...The theme of the Aryan World Congress was the urgent need
for white people
to establish an independent homeland,
apart from jews, blacks, gay people, and other
minority groups
that supremacists blame
for an erosion of
American
Culture ... .

American. Culture. Solemn. Cross. Burning. Service. Gathered to
dismantle the practices established to address exclusionary
processes. the urgent need. Tribalism. American. Culture. White.

167

Supremacists from around the country and Canada gathered.
Exclusionary. Solemn. apart from jews, blacks, gay people, and
other minority groups. and other. and other. and other. and
brother. mother. other exclusionary processes. dismantle the
practices. Solemn. Erosion. jews, blacks, gay people, and other
minority groups. gathered. University of California Regents
gathered. the urgent need for white people. University of
California Regents gathered to dismantle the practices established
to address exclusionary processes

... The compound,
with its tall Aryan Nation sign,
is accessible
by driving
several hundred yards up
a winding gravel road,
where the most prominent
sign is one instructing visitors, *Whites Only.*

Whites Only.
Whites Only.

To dismantle the practices established to address exclusionary processes
Whites Only.

Campuses	(erosion)
with their tall iron gates	(solemn)
remain open to all	(gathered)
but not accessible.	(exclusionary)
How does one outlast	(burning)
a winding path	(affirmative)
of unequal opportunity?	(action)

What If God Is a Creep?

What if God is a creep
who wishes He was taller
who didn't get the girl
who picks on people
not His own size?
What if God laughed
when Jesus had
second thoughts?
What if His sense of order
is no more complex
than kids playing
King of the Hill
or Smear the Queer?

What if God is really a creep
who beats His wife
embezzles when He can
and jerks off to violent porn?
Perhaps God put Darwin on earth
to help us understand
that the very traits of man
which survive the longest
and determine the fittest
are God's own favorite attributes?
Maybe He's a boss who expects favors
a professor who makes others feel stupid
a witness obstructing justice.

What if God is really just a creep?
Maybe Machiavelli was
His inspired son
and *The Prince*
remains our most sacred text.
What if Hitler sits
at God's right hand
tended by a heavenly host
of bigots, bullies, soldiers
and other serial killers

who look to an angel
named Manson
for advice.

A God capable of
biological brilliance
and genetic genius
is no more likely to care
about justice and kindness
than His creations are.
Why assume that
God likes women
any more than men do?
Why imagine
He wouldn't hurt His children?

God's morality might be just
as steeped in struggle
as accented by abuse
as spiced with exploitation
and as baked in brutality
as our own common recipes.
Drink up.
One taste
and you are
in Heaven.

If God really is
a creep
that certainly would
explain
a lot.

Willing

I believe the dog walkers
as they point to the spot
on the bay where they say
they have just seen
a whale.

"It was on the news last night,"
the owner of a black lab
assures me
and I take her words
to be true.

I have no doubt
that somewhere
under the restless surface
swims a graceful humpback
or a finner.

And though I've never seen a whale
in the wild
I am content
to spy a common sea lion
swimming close to shore.

I jog along
as the sea lion sweeps through the surf beside me
keeping my pace
or me
keeping hers

parallel paths
one afoot
one afloat
as the sleek nose
pokes through the foamy tide to air

followed by a wide and gleaming back
arching
sliding
gliding with equal measure

before giving way to the slap of its tail.

A small patch of splash
appeared at steady intervals
then disappeared
as quickly.
The sea lion left no trail.

She just rose and dove again
to the undertow
to the world below
that I am forever
stranger to.

Still, the others said,
a whale was out there.
And I believed them.
I know
how easy it is

to hide
the elephant
in a small room
to see the mouse nibbling cheese
at the foot of a rising mountain.

I know
how little it takes
to disguise
heartache
with a smile.

An enormous whale
in a shallow bay—
everyone saw it
but me.
And I believed

what I wanted to
believe.
I was running
with one
who was willing.

Yet Another Paradise Lost

Our sleepy dead end road
doubled as a baseball field
or street hockey rink
depending on the season.
Cars waited patiently
or impatiently
as we sighed
in annoyance
reluctantly moving
the nets or bases
and stepping just far enough aside
for drivers to inch by.

Adults ruled the houses
and the yards
but the streets
the woods
and the swamp
were ours.
Algae fights transcended
pecking order:
Poised on our fleet of rafts
we poled out to the marshy tufts
scooped up green slime
and hurled away.
Some days we had teams
but mostly it was free-for-all.
Everyone got picked on at some point
the quasi-compliment of being singled out
that came with the territory
as if to say
we tease you, therefore, you are one of us.
If someone got hurt or went home crying
the rest felt bad
admitted we had gone too far
and tried to make amends.
A day hardly ever went by
when someone didn't say
"I'm sorry."

VIII. MEASUREMENT

Start Testing

Pragmatism: *the truth of a concept can be deter-
mined by testing it against experimental results
and practical consequences.*

what results if we ... touch. fly. fall. flaunt.
pry. feel. laugh. haunt. steal. fold. veer.
hold. speak. pray. leave. fight. stay. stand.
stray. bite. crash. command. swerve.
breathe. yearn. demand. unnerve. land.
dare. jump. believe. don't.

Time and Distance

the destination
math lesson:
the countdown
a decade
the diver's perfect score
the decathlete's challenge
Odysseus's quest
Commandments
the ten-minute ascent
ten toes
ten fingers
every metric measurement
depending on
days
between

of the first
10
marking lift off
a dime
the sides on a decagon
the faces of a decahedron
for home
handed down in stone
of Athena rising from sea foam
maybe mine
certainly yours
everything
ten
the time
us

The Bridges of Marin County

harbor views back east
never so panoramic
but here

driving the folds
of mt tamalpais
the whole picture smooth

blue of the bay
set like a table
for dinner guests who seat themselves

in berkeley oakland and san jose
pass around delicate dishes
of angel island ferry boats and alcatraz

i'll save a spot for you
in san francisco spread
with your favorite dishes

don't leave me
hanging in marin
dinner at eight and everyone else

on time
you said you'd bring the wine
we waited

as long as we could
the food
went cold

witnesses said
that you stood
nearly an hour

i imagine you crossing
back and forth

leaning tower to tower

finally
choosing
the southern

your wish to rest
nearer the city
than the driveway

how long had you been letting
your two selves push each other over
the edge

stuffing your pockets
with secrets and shame
weighing yourself down

with cement shoes
a gangster assuring your own
silence

i pay the toll daily
wondering
as the dark shroud

of the bay
smoothed over you
that night

who did you think
your quiet splash
was saving

were you keeping
yourself from the pleasures
you found in the city

boys in dark bars
handsome men who loved you
did they love you too

did you wrestle with vertigo
lose your sense of balance
imagine yourself icarus

dizzied by your own precarious perch
glorious ride
on flawed wings

was it so impossible to live
and love on both sides
of the bay

did you think i couldn't feel
your love
when it was there for me

your distraction
when desires
divided

history like the water
smoothes over
with half-truth

story of good job
and grieving widow
but each time i cross

this span
i wonder
about the men

with whom i share the loss
of you
invisibly

i sit unseen in
a castro cafe
wondering which men

gave you what kinds

of comfort
delight

satisfaction
these men of leather
metal tattoos

did you know them
how did you get their attention
how did they get yours

did you walk hand-in-hand
with a man who looked like you
the marlboro man double exposed

did you bury a love of bondage
dominance submission
in the bay

did you find friendship too
would you and i have found
the same men handsome

where are you
in this cafe crowd
i want to love

what you wouldn't show
me
dance with more than

a slice of truth
hold your halves together
in my arms

and rock them till i have mourned
and honored
the whole of you

was it so impossible to
cross that divide

to live

and love
on both sides
of the bay

hey
isn't that what bridges
are for

Your Words

intimate
intrusive
embedded

your words
a puppy's tongue
too strong a wind
a rusted nail

i love you
too

At the Buzzer

Standing on the sideline
like an editor's note in the margin
I watch the team make a mockery
of the X's and O's I scrawled at the half.

I blind myself to the third consecutive turnover
a stupid foul and an easy lay-up missed by my star forward.
As the final minute ticks away
the scoreboard is kind enough to give us hope.

When we somehow cut the lead to one
my reflexes signal "time-out."
Brain cells sprint from one endline to the other
in search of a comeback play to win this at the buzzer.

Efforts to locate the play are lost
in the weave of so many games in so many years
and the shouts of the tallest girl on the team
screaming in my ear.

The roar from the bleachers drowns out
the southern drawl of my gentle giant
            (who is as stooped in her shoulders
            as she is long in her legs
            who is unable to catch a ball
            you place in her hands
            who sits the entire game
            all season beside me
            cheering and heaping encouragement
            on her teammates
            who nods her head in excited agreement
            at every word I say)
who now grabs my arm, excited:
"Coach! Coach! I know a play!"

The seriousness and exhilaration in her words
remind me of the eager "yes, ma'am" she sang
every time I sent her in

(only when we had an 18-point lead).

I know how I'm supposed to react
how the reins are mine
how coaches should be field marshals
and here it is a clutch moment

And I am interrupted by a bench warmer
the backup
to the backup center
the last girl to survive cuts.

My face burns red.
The spit of past coaches mists my forehead
and I hear their shouts
carried on a pitch which humiliates fully.

I once took pride in being the rare player
who knew how to endure a coach's tirade.
I ran harder, longer, and played on a sprain all winter—
anything that might earn me a splinter of praise.

"Coach, I know a play!"
She hasn't repeated the phrase,
but it is still hanging in the air between us
and I don't know what to say

To this girl who calls me "Coach"
as if the title comes with a palace and a crown.
I retreat to a mental search for the choreography
that will guarantee victory.

The bench leaps up to greet
the sweaty five returning from action.
The six-footer with bent shoulders
turns her attention from me

To slap palms with the starting center.
"Way to go!" she urges
and then looks back in my direction
eyes pleading with me to let her tell her plan.

Five panting girls stand waiting for their orders.
A spot is cleared for me in the heart of the huddle.
Prepared to draw my X's and O's
and send them on their mission

I look up at the starters
but in each I see
the eyes of the one who says
she knows a play.

I am shouting "You can do it!"
not so sure if they can
as the circle breaks in a concert of cheers.
My silence has already spoken for me.

I knelt wordlessly
nodding and listening
as the backup to the backup center
diagrammed our final play.

Five take to the floor, triumph on their minds.
Eight more are lined beside me
on their feet, holding hands
and breathless in their shared but silent prayer

That our final shot will fall.
I scan the eager faces of these young women
who have woven themselves
into a wishful chain.

A pair of stooped shoulders
rises
to the rafters
like a championship banner.

The young woman lifts herself above us all.
The scoreboard fades. The last-second shot will
or will not fall. The buzzer will sound.
The victory has already been posted.

The Clock Strikes

a dozen eggs, fragile, like love
a dozen ears of corn, thanksgiving
a dozen donuts, sweet
 (i am hungry for you)
twelve inches to a foot
twelve jurors in the box
twelve hours on a clock face
(if we were sequestered in a small space for days on end how
        would we pass the time?)
the twelve strokes of midnight
(can you feel how strong the pounding of my heart tonight
as I fall to sleep
thinking of you?)

Where We Met

Gravity had an extra hold on him, but he had the strength of a Titan. The ball was too bouncy for his thick-fingered hands. Sometimes, his whole body went on strike, just walked out on him, left him to spasm and thrash as classmates looked on, laughed, and gave him nicknames he had to pretend to like.

They thought he was stupid, but he knew that he was just slow, needed things repeated. He always understood what mattered most: the difference between kind and unkind.

It would have been easy for him to resent the grace and agility that others possessed. But he gloried in those who had what he lacked. He discovered the men who could make all men cheer, the giants of sport. Through their exploits he entered a fast-paced world that he could keep up with—numbers, names, legends, and games. He wore a football helmet with the face guard removed to keep him safe in a seizure, but it also protected the treasures he stored: batting orders, final scores, yards rushed, and records broken. He possessed the sweaty data lovingly and offered tidbits of legends and leagues as gifts to others who wanted to share in his strength rather than his weakness.

Even as an adult, the boy within him ruled. He peppered people with his sports trivia, quizzed anyone who would listen, and he did whatever it took to stand court side: swept the floor, carried towels, brought water. The only thanks he ever asked were to be close to the action, to savor excitement, to cheer the plays, and to call a team his own.

So, we met in the gym. I was a freshman shooting baskets. He had just finished sweeping the floor. He stood watching, then offered to rebound. He immediately started in like a broadcaster, narrating my moves, announcing my shooting drills. He created a game around my private workout, making me the star, christening me with a dozen nicknames—all this in an era when nobody watched women's basketball.

So our paths converged on the hardwood. Though we did not start with shared expectations, we found words to explain our friendship. I overheard him tell someone that I was his girlfriend. At first he was hurt when I told him not to call me that. I scolded him like a child. But his protests, so thoughtful and genuine, made me see the flaw in my presumption that I could control what he felt. We agreed to call each other pals. So, pals it was and pals we stayed.

Aside from my family and two high school friends, he was the only person I invited to my college graduation. Two hours earlier than I told him to come by, he announced his arrival: *"It's Mr. Sports himself, live on the banks of the Charles, ready to bring you the excitement of today's graduation!"* I tried to find vertical balance, holding off the sting of the night's revels. I opened my dorm door to his wide smiled and a massive cake with "Congratulations, Pal!" scripted in sugar. As always, a plea for approval followed: *"Bet you thought it was really Howard Cosell, didn't you?"*

It wasn't easy drawing lines. I knew that I couldn't believe everything he told me. Sometimes he believed his own wishful thinking. Sometimes his memory failed him—but never around sports. I took in all he offered, trying as best I could to imagine the rest. He sensed being different, longed to fit in. When he phoned late at night to talk of not having the kind of job that makes you a somebody in this world, it was my turn to be his fan. I listened and tried to rebound for him, offered pep talks as best I could. I always hung up to an echo of those words: "Thanks, Coach," or "Buddy" or "Pal."

A handshake or high-five could light him up like a scoreboard. He taught me to revel in a moment, to look past the obvious, to open myself to all the forms love takes. He taught me to trust what is good and not just what is convenient, and he kept my belief in heroes alive.

"I have tickets for tonight's game from one of my friends on the team," he'd boast. One of your friends? The team? I'd be dubious. But then there we were at Boston Garden with great seats, his stories rolling about how he knew so-and-so from his playing days at such-and-such college. Where he used to sweep, carry towels, bring water ...

He'd insist that we visit the locker room where, sure enough, the superstar source of our tickets emerged all showered and towering above us, pausing to greet my pal by name, ask how he'd been, how were the seats. And all because some other players who befriended him in other gyms eventually turned pro. The ones who made time for him turned hero in my book for demonstrating the humanity that statistics and news stories never record.

He took up swimming in his thirties and found a new freedom as he cut through the water. To feel his body pull, kick, and glide in lightness and speed was to feel the superstar in himself emerge. He discovered ways to measure improvement, to set his sights on the clock and not worry about who was in the next lane.

Between childhood and manhood he learned the lesson that so many athletes overlook: that winning has more to do with the individual than with the competition. And what a rare individual he was thrashing through the water, looking on the bright side, making the most of what life served him. He sang the lyrics of sports everywhere, jingling the jock jargon in his pockets, lavishing every description with sports lingo. To hear him cast a cliché was to hear the freshest set of words in the world. It was as if the players and their games promised him something as simple and splendid as the stars.

Once he said to me: *If I can't marry you, could we work a basketball camp together someday? Wouldn't that be great, you and me, coaching together?* He sure knew how to put life in perspective. And when I last saw him, he said, *"I know you can't be, but I wish you were my wife or my sister."* And I tried to put it in perspective for both of us: "That's why we're pals."

No, our friendship was never conventional. Everything about him transcended convention, even the athlete. What he lacked in quickness and agility, he more than made up for with his simple grace and optimism.

His life ended early and mostly unnoticed—no sneakers named for him, no number retired, no Hall of Fame vote. But those of us who traded high-fives with him, who knew his play-by-play accounts of a game's final drama, we were changed for the better by his passion and his drive. He was the friendliest of fighters, the most loyal of fans, and the kindest of competitors—all because his heart was by far his most powerful and talented muscle.

In Training

I tried to teach my new dog
an old trick or two
but she was uninterested in orthodoxy.

No room for roll over.
No patience for fetch.
Nothing but eat, sleep, romp and stretch.

My perky pooch took me under her furry wing
and taught me the canine order of things.
In short, she gave me the scoop.

I was taught that "sit"
means to chase one's tail,
that "come" means bark or poop.

Then I learned that the point of a trail
is to know where to stray from,
and that leashes, no matter the length,

should be wadded and stuffed in a pocket.
The next lesson, don't mock it, was this:
If there's an itch, scratch.

I am no match for her.
Whoever said that you can't teach an old dog
a new trick

hasn't met my little escapee from the pound
because that mutt has found
thousands of tricks to teach little old me.

Every Hour More

for DSA

Better than the mind
the body knows
what it's like
not to

what it's like
not to
do
that which it has done

tirelessly
repeatedly
lovingly
painfully

at times, perhaps,
mechanically,
if only to dull
the blade.

A body knows what it's like
not to do
that which it has
done

(not to stir the orange juice
not to read aloud in stillness
not to watch the breathing
not to laugh self-consciously

not to hear
his laughter)
how can it feel like anything
but loss

the glass drained
the air stilled
the pills useless
the pages unturned

the hand not there
to hold
nothing holds
not even an echo.

Did you ever imagine that an emptiness could fill
a room
a house
your own body

like a loud silence
a visible darkness
a paradox of loss
that leaves you with a tangible nothingness.

It's more than
being without
and it's staring at you
from his favorite chair

weighing on you
like sandbags
in moments least expected
barricades give way

to floods
that fill
your whole being
with negative lead.

So usurped by what is no more
you think the air has been drained from the sky
the light pushed out of your lungs
your limbs turned inside out.

All as you knew it

departed
with the arrival
of his absence

but something didn't stop
when the breathing did
and that's what you
are left with

the something in you
that kept pulsing
something of him
settling in.

You finally understand
negative numbers
all those years in school
never understanding

that line above the blackboard
how there could be less
than nothing
3 ... 2 ... 1 ... 0 ... -1 ... -2 ...

and every hour
more still
still more
emptiness

more absence
more missing him
more of him missing
something else you think you might understand now: infinity.

Loss pouring itself
into a loss
all that loss
all that loss gathering in one place

lining up on hangers
folding in between the sheets

sneaking under the cans in the pantry
sliding sideways amid the books shelved in the den

ticket stubs, post cards, photographs and horoscopes
priceless scraps folded into your wallet
with the priceless hope
of something to hold on to.

Call it a loss
but claim it
collect it
frame it

then carry it
not a burden
not a load
but a collection

of jewels
sparkling like words
for you alone
to wear:

the ruby of his vigor
the moonstone of his bravado
the amethyst of his fight
the diamond of his wisdom.

It can only feel like a loss
but your very presence
is him
in you

he leaves eight children
he leaves two daughters
he leaves …
they got it wrong

he did not simply leave
did not leave you
on the top step
alone.

He has left himself
in you
he has left you
in charge

of his magic
to conjure
smiles
and laughter.

He has left you
conversant in joy
well-versed in whimsy
fluent in honesty.

You are heir
to his integrity
his passion
his strength.

He has left you the keys
he has left you
the enormous task
of sharing him.

Of course you can't see it
any more than you can see
the straightening of your teeth
or the strengthening of your spine

but smile and stand tall
knowing that you can still lean
on him, call him
your backbone.

Repeat Offender

I am the perpetual
prodigal
the itinerant
sister
the one who keeps
returning
with no basket of gifts
without jewels in hand
not even a bottle of wine
I arrive on my own time with
holes in my empty pockets
a hollow wallet
abandoned dreams
and bandages holding together
a depleted heart

Charred by deserts willingly walked
blistered and shoeless
I return
belted by hunger
with my shirt
tattered and stained
my soul heavily
weathered
by more than the rain.

In short,
my tank has been fully drained.

Yet you besiege me
with greetings
and joy

Doors swing wide without hesitation
unequivocal arms open again
clean sheets are turned down for me
and the finest cutlery
is set out with fanfare and celebration

again

In the far corner of the barn
another fatted calf
trembles

I have found
my way
to you
again
I have found my way
home

And
you have found
a way to
love
me
again
and
again

IX. CONTRADICTION

Concurrent

Pluralism: *separate and independent levels of reality exist.*

same room. same day. same window. scrub jay. nuthatch. junco. they lounge together on the couch. fire. fog. hum. bills to pay. one feels a longing. laundry drying. the other longs to feel. same window. one sees the other's reflection. who looks beyond the glass to the shifting patch of shade where a hummingbird hangs and lifts its beak to feed. recollection of words exchanged at a flower stand. laundry to fold. never been to Peru. will I grow old alone? what was it that the artist said about the conflict of form and memory? did I invest wisely? hunger. corner store. hunger. ground water. hunger. rest. paint peeling. read Chekhov. blue. rebellion. desire. the ceiling. collect butterfly wings. They lounge. buyer's market. together. seller's market. on the couch. same room. same day. same window. different hungers.

Casey As He Sat

Part I: 1890   There is no joy in Mudville,
but I won't take the blame.
Sure, I might have hit the long shot
that would have won the game.

But I won't play the loser.
I'm sweaty and satisfied.
The crowd can boo and hiss at me,
but they cannot take my pride.

I'm no source of evil,
just a gentle, hard-working guy.
I play for love of the game,
not for what a fan can buy.

If home runs make men smile,
then let them hit some of their own.
Only then will they feel the thrill I feel
When my bat rips through the zone.

The ripples that run through me
When my homers clear the yard
cannot be hawked like peanuts
or shelled out like trading cards.

The highest peak of a hitting streak
is not lessened by the hurt
of whiffing on an outside curve
or fanning in the dirt.

To fail in this sweet game
is to let the innings pass you by.
There's always victory in knowing that
you gave it your best try.

So if bands aren't marching merrily,
if Mudville isn't singing,
I'll still whistle my winner's tune
because at least I struck out swinging.

Part II: 1990   You say "no joy in Mudville."
Why should I give a flyin' stitch?
I would have hit the game-winner
if I'd seen a decent pitch.

Don't hang this loss on my head.
I won't be your chump.
If they want to blame somebody,
let 'em blame the ump!

I work my butt off every day.
I don't get any rest.
This crowd doesn't support me.
How can I perform my best?

I'm going to Disneyland.
I'm not the play-off goat.
I've got a five-year contract.
I've got a mile-long boat.

I know that I'm a winner,
I thank the good Lord every day.
If I were any kind of a sinner
would I be so blessed to play?

If God grants me the strength some days
to hit to the left field bleachers,
let the folks in the stands rejoice
and admire my better features.

Some days my timing's off
I don't come through in the clutch.
My fans should be more realistic.
They're expecting way too much.

There's no one who likes more to win,
to finish in first place.
I got myself a six-figure bonus
when we won the pennant race.

Let 'em trash me on talk radio.
Let Mudville drown its sorrow.
Lighten up—it's a seven-game series.
I'll be in my groove tomorrow.

Dog Eat Dog World

You look lovely tonight
and the world is lovely too
except
        for the newborn pit bull
                dangling from a chain
                        puppy peddling blindly to nowhere
                                suspended bait for the snarling hounds below
                                        whose hunger pangs have been patiently cultivated
                                        and carefully honed for the past few days
                                                by a man who complains
                                                        that his dinner is cold.
                                                My only wish is to love you,
                                        to be loved. So let us leave
                                our scarred lives
                        at the door
                ride the wind
            and fish the sky
        for stars
        that don't
bite.

Trading

Trading was low today.
Look for a rise in interest rates.
Technicians registered a slight drop this quarter.
Experts say the market may continue to fluctuate.

Look for a rise in interest rates.
The time is right for an outlandish adventure.
Don't underestimate the value of old friends.
Your sensuality may surprise you.

The time is right for an outlandish adventure.
We've got just the package you're looking for.
Prices have never been better
and terrorism is down.

We've got just the package you're looking for
A time-share in Mexico
with American food and bottled water for you
And our staff speaks excellent English.

Look for a rise; the time is right.
We've got just the package:
Your sensuality and terrorism bottled
Experts say the market may continue to fluctuate.

That's All

A fully indulged Jack
Russell Terrier
off leash
and teasing a much larger
hound

bounds toward me
as if without owner
I bend to see if
the dog will stop to greet me.
It runs right by.

"Look what you've done now,"
chastises a voice
from behind me
and I gather the dog
is in trouble.

But, no,
it is at me
the fiery silver eyes narrow
as the old lady repeats
"Look what you've done."

I am not sure what I have done
to deserve such rancor
but I am the object of her British scorn.
"'E would never 'ave run like that
if not for you," she admonishes me, emphasis on *you*.

Though I disagree
I say nothing,
stunned in the face of a face
that surely belongs to someone's grandmother,
a face etched with age and squinting with irritation.

This sturdy English lady
slightly bent in timelessness

does not know how her white hair dances
along the edges of her crocheted cap
or how the sun behind shines through to form a silky halo.

Still, she wields her walking
stick like a scepter
or a spear
as she marches along the footpath
by Folly's Bridge

(a ritual she began
I am sure
long before I was born).
She is strong and
patient in her able stride

and I am clearly wrong
for thinking to interfere
with her little dog
and by extension
her daily routine.

I apologize as
earnestly and efficiently as I can
and walk on
unaware that the path ends
just ahead.

When I reach the locked gate I turn
uneasy in the knowledge that I will pass
this woman, her dog,
and I hope not her wrath,
again.

As they approach
the dog leads in eager gallop
and I make no eye contact
no gesture that might
catch canine interest.

The dog runs by

and I try to hide my relief.
Then I notice the notice
the woman takes in me.
What a stare.

So, I stare back
in wonder at her wonder.
Our eyes take hold. Our heads turn.
As we align,
she stops. I stop.

We face off,
her armor a different vintage and design than mine.
An overcoat and thick-heeled shoes for her.
Black leather jacket
and bleached-out, two-toned hair for me.

But there is a safety
in the distance between us.
We stand in silent freeze
at the center of a path
that she considers hers.

I am the foreigner here.
She has seen many wars.
"I couldn't tell," she says with a hint of accusation
"if you were a man
or a woman—that's all."

I say nothing,
smile a little
at my surprise
to hear her say,
"that's all."

"Your hair, it's unnatural," she adds.
Unnatural? I think to myself
wondering how much of a bridge
we can build
between us.

"So are our clothes,"
I want to say "shall we take them off?"
But of course I don't say that.
"I like it," I say
of my hair.

"It doesn't suit you,"
she says. So I ask
"What do you think
would suit me?" and I am keen
to hear her answer.

An awkward pause grows between us
then subsides
as we both recognize
how unable she is to fathom just what would
suit me.

She retreats to what she knows.
"I haven't done that to my hair
and look what nature has done.
It's curly," she says
patting her fragile halo.

As unconvinced as I am,
she adds a last word
as if its finality will make her right:
"It doesn't suit you,
that's all."

And that's how we left it,
that was all.
Though I still wonder
exactly how
she tells it.

What The Cat Contemplates While Pretending to Clean Herself

So attentive
to her paws
she seems
leaning over
licking
tirelessly
but thinking
not about what dirt
has climbed under her claws.
No, the cat sees herself
sternly stepping to the plate
spitting in her paw palms
and gripping the bat just so.
With a look of feline indifference
she tends to one final itch
before staring down the pitcher
in the last instant before delivery.

When she rubs
her wet cat wrist
behind her furry ear
you'd think she had a spot
of mud there
or a flea
but really
the cat is signaling
the runner at first
to stretch that lead a little further down the baseline.

By the time
she is perched
on her hind legs
lapping at the fur
of her underside
the cat is sliding safely
into home.

Prospects

Let it rain rain rain
29 points per game
raining buckets
over hard city
pavement pivot
to the hole
bury it bury it
inside outside
nothing but net
bury it bury
the jumper
swish
      swish
         swish

Scouting Report:
impact player has it all
inside strength outside
touch speed vision range
finds/creates openings
penetrates with confidence
unstoppable

Invite the double team
then dish
Let em gang up
create any mismatch
you won't be denied
give-and-go
2-on-1 to the hole
nobody stops you
slam bam
on rival schools
to the tune of 29
a game
have your way
on the boards
follow your shot
second chance
rebound
off the glass
two more
run hook
post up

Coaches calling calling
calling
courting that jumper
gonna make six-foot-five
Richie a star
ring-ring-ring
Coach Blaney
Richie a household name
ring-ring
         Coach Majerus
Richie in Nike
Richie rich
    Coach Jarvis
ring ring ring
championship ring
Richie Parker Richie Parker
shooting guard
six-foot-five Richie Parker
scholarship offers
choices choices choices
free ride

stick it   meal ticket
stick the J   promises promises promises
love to stick   ring   ring   rings
that jumper—   no strings attached
swish   promises promises
        swish   nobody stops you
            swish   promises

*"I want to go to college
get good grades
and play ball."*

                            studious sophomore
                            fifteen years old
                            same hard city pavement
                            no jumper
                            except the one she wears
                            wants to go to college
                            become a doctor
                            can't post up
                            fifteen years old
                            can't find her locker
                            between classes

long checkered hallways   The Louisiana Purchase

girls giggling with gossip   promises promises promises

book bags and barrettes   guys slapping each other on the

watch your   back

playing rap   IF 2>1.5 AND 1.5>1 THEN 2>1

in tape decks

    i wish i was taller   Theorem

    i wish i was a baller   Corollary

    i wish i had a girl so i could call her   Proof

bells between classes   crusty chemistry labs

not exactly the paved road   matter cannot be created

to Harvard but

room to believe in   nor destroyed

becoming a doctor

if only she could find
her way back to
civics class   civ · ics / *n pl but sing or pl in*
                                 construction: a social science
                                 dealing with the rights
                                 and duties
                                 of citizens

Coach Jarvis: "I don't recruit anybody if I don't think they're a
great person and they can't come and contribute not just to our
school but to our society."

if only she could find

                                                    if only
                                              she could find
                                                    her way
                                                   her word
                                                    if only
                                                   her word
                                                against his

                and who knows what was said

[*Hey, baby. Where you headed?*   create openings
    Hey, girl.
The two of us, you stick with us   double team
    Yeah, stick with us.
We'll show you around   mismatch
around around a round
a round and thick   "great person"
in the stairwell

round and thick   2-on-1
Suck this
Suck this   2 > 1
Suck this]
                                   give-and-go
limited choices
                                   rights and duties
what kind of offer
                                   can't be denied
to the tune of 29 points a game

CHARGE: first-degree sodomy   SENTENCE: five years probation
plead guilty   "not just to our school"
to first-degree sexual abuse   looking at a four-year offer

                "come and contribute"

CHARGE: top prospect
    six-foot-five
    penetrates
    with confidence
    29 a game
    unstoppable   SENTENCE: "but to our society"

                    Headlines scream
                       writers rant
                      lawyers settle
                     Richie apologizes
                    promises promises
                   haunted by hallway
                                        [midnight storms
                                              suck this
                                              bury it
                                    let it rain rain rain]

college high road
offers rescinded
coaches urge understanding:
"This girl could have damaged
Parker for life.
Five years from now
this will haunt
him ... "

                              [midnight storms
                                    suck this
                                     bury it
                        let it rain rain rain]

" ... a mistake;
they shouldn't have been there. But everyone's worried
about the girl.
What about him?"

                                    worried
                            everyone's worried
                    the girl the girl about the girl
                everyone's worried about the girl
                                   everyone

"we recruit good people." "She believes Richie is sincere when he
says he is sorry." "what you plead guilty to and what transpired
were different things from what I've come to believe." "Because
he's a nice person." "I do understand women's victimization. If it
were my wife or daughters" "not everybody who pleads guilty is
always guilty." "At what point should the punitive measures end?"
"unbalanced publicity" "Everybody deserves another shot." "She
accepts his apology."

everyone's worried everyone coach jarvis coach majerus coach blaney
coach coach coach everyone
everyone's worried about the girl.

What about him?

        "They didn't take a chance to look at me as a person."

the girl the girl the girl a chance a person the girl
        (who was heckled out of their high school
                        then from the next as if it were her fault
                        now on her third school since the assault
                        suffocation nightmares
                        still wants to go to college
                        be a doctor
                        high price to pay

                    for being in the wrong stairwell
                        for blowing the whistle
                            for crying "Foul"
                                for tattling on
                                    the basketball star)

cit·i·zen·ship / *n.* 1: status of being a citizen 2: the quality of an
individual's response to membership in a community

At what point should the punitive measures end?
                                            [midnight storms
                                                suck this
                                                    bury it
                                        let it rain rain rain]

(AP)—George Washington
University officials say a
scholarship offer to a 17-
year-old student is not re-
lated to her sexual assault
by a basketball player the
college is recruiting.

                                        unbalanced publicity

            Everybody deserves another shot

Increments

a poem discovered
with my ninth grade students

By the questions asked
answers are revealed.
By anger implied
rage comes to life.

       A small scale
       cannot weigh
       the mountain's age

A lizard's eye
cannot follow
an eagle's path.

          Why does one
          try to measure
          another?

     The kestrel nests
     A dog curls by the fire
     Bees tend to their queen
     I smile. I live. I desire.

       All measuring instruments have their own
                       limitations.
         So too
               do the measurements
                 they yield.

Be sure to hold past the breaking point until the next ceiling is revealed.
Map
the edges
to know what waits
beyond.
       Calibrate restraint.

Let the ones who measure me
be air
enough
liquid enough
fire enough.

One Branch

My great-great-grandmother Rosina
was born just as the Erie Canal
was opening upstate to the ocean.
She was only four when she started traveling
with her daddy through the northern Adirondacks
selling snake skins, ground bones and cactus sap.
Rosina loved to bathe in icy mountain runoff,
and though people scoffed,
she developed an obsession for waterfalls.
By sixteen she was an experienced barrel queen.

They say that she would have been the first
to run Niagara Falls
if she hadn't gone fishing near Keene.
The grass was tall and scorched brown that July
but the bass were biting like hungry house flies.
Most men along the trails were heading west
in the rush for gold
but not the soulful Bernard Knittel.
Relatives tell how he cast his line where he sat
on the steamy shores of Lake Saranac

And Rosina Shorer bit.
"Why go west," he is said to have said,
"when there's no purer gold
than the handhold of a beautiful Rose like you."
And on that note, everyone knows,
he touched her left earlobe and for the first time
she blushed. Bernard Knittel rushed from his knees
to offer not a ring but an engagement bracelet.
They say he braided it on the spot
of hopsack and daisies.

Rosina, being an unusual lady,
suggested they smoke a cigar
to seal the deal.
Still puffing away on a stogie
she let him slip the bracelet on her wrist

and the fish went ignored for the rest of the day.
Only after my great-great-grandfather died
did Rosina decide
that her husband of forty one years
had been part Indian.

First, there was the prophetic fact
that his arrival on god's Earth
coincided with the bureaucratic birth
of the Indian Removal Act.
There was also something tangible,
Rosina reasoned, in the way the seasons turned
around him. He often talked to the fish he caught,
tossing the young ones back to the lake
so they could meet again at a later date.
"Even fish deserve long life," Bernie once told his wife.

Their only daughter, Mary Theresa,
arrived in Ilion, New York
amid the boil of the Civil War.
Bernard refused to fight for either side
citing a dislike of both
slavery and the so-called Union.
The way Rosina told it
something mysterious took
my great-great-granddaddy's life
on the very day that Crazy Horse was killed.

"Something in his heart refused to carry on
carving up the country.
He always said we all was traitors to the hills
and living on first-degree stolen land.
He must have been part Indian."
That's how Rosina saw it
just before she died in 1914
death being the only thing that stopped her
from marching with Emma Goldman and Belva Lockwood.
So in her place her only daughter made the trip.

Mary marched
yet never felt the part of a suffragette.

Still, she couldn't forget
what her mother had said
about her father being Indian.
And when the government declared
all Native Americans "aliens,"
Mary cashed in her savings bonds
slashed the tires on the sheriff's car
and set fire to the Ithaca town hall.

Mary met a Canadian trapper
with a smooth Halifax accent
whose name rhymed with *freeway*.
They say that Enos LeBoutilier
proposed with the hope that they would elope.
But Mary, eager enough to kiss Ithaca good-bye,
was reluctant to leave her friends behind.
So Enos made a guest list for the trip
wired relatives in Naragansett
and organized a group elopement to Woonsocket.

Enos was a hunting man
who reluctantly punched a clock
long hours at the loading dock.
Somewhere in that marriage
the Franco-prefix fell by the Catskill wayside
and LeBoutilier (which rhymed with *stray*)
moved nearer the front of the alphabet
as Enos Boutilier (rhyming now with *chandelier*)
moved nearer the front
of the paycheck line.

First Monday of every month
Enos wired money to his parents.
He visited them once a year
in Nova Scotia
and would have fallen
into a wanderer's despair
to hear of the violent deaths
that stole their lives away
when a steel-sided ship
exploded in Halifax Harbor one day.

But Enos himself
had already died a decade earlier
without any particular fanfare or fame.
Within a fortnight of Enos's passing
his brother Amos took up the family flame
by marrying my widowed great-grandmother.
Amos might have taken the time then
to map the family tree
for his nieces-and-nephews turned step-children
but he didn't.

If ever the young ones
sought first-hand knowledge
of their French-Canadian roots
they found that all province records
of Edward LeBoutilier
and his Hudson Bay wife
Isabelle Wynaught
were lost in the same flames
of the maritime explosion
that claimed their lives.

Then just as Orville and Wilbur
were getting off the ground in Kitty Hawk
life crashed down on Amos and Mary.
They lost three sons in one year when
eight-year-old Franklin drowned
at a quarry near Pixley Falls
then Bernie and Eddy
got caught on the railroad bridge
just as the 4:05 was arriving
ten minutes early from Albany.

Life stayed on track
for the remaining three—
William, Robert, and their sister Alice,
named for the girl with the Cheshire cat.
The youngest
the only daughter
Alice had no use for a looking glass.
She was society's stranger

with a temper short as a mosquito's eyelash
and as dangerous as Horseshoe Falls.

They say she ruled Palmyra's pool halls
gambling when she wasn't stealing
dancing when she wasn't dealing.
She liked her meat cooked
but only on one side.
Breakfast was always brown rice,
prunes and a sprinkle of Chinese herb.
Her brother William claimed
that Alice's fame was teaching Annie Oakley
to whistle through her teeth.

In the turn of a calendar
Utah became a state
giving the flag its forty-fifth star
separate but equal became law
and Alice became big sister
to Robert Amos Boutilier.
Years after Amelia Earhart
disappeared over the Pacific
Alice told her kid brother
to visit the Great Salt Lake.

By then he had married
one of the Williams sisters
stubborn Welsh women with strong backs and thin fingers.
Ellis Island had been her family's gate to fortune
but young Ruth found her own destiny
with a gentle gunsmith
who snored like a seagull
laughed like Benny Goodman
danced the Charleston unevenly
and lived to be called Grampa by me.

The family tree should grow firmer here.
Grampa's workbench
        where I learned to work a crescent wrench and read a spirit level.
Grampa's gun rack
        where I discovered the difference between smooth and rifled-bore
                barrels.

History should be easier as the memories grow more tangible.
Grampa's shuffle
     the walk that wore the carpet thin in our living room.
Grampa's hands
     age-stiffened claws that ran through white thinning hair
          when he grew confused.

Not much of an heirloom today,
the two half-sheets
of paper
I treasure
stapled to a postcard that reads:
Vacation ends tonight.
Good trip. Great weather.
First week at the Cape,
Second, New York State.
Love, your father

The date hardly makes it a relic—August 1991.
The prose
is less than poetic
but in familiar script:
P.S. I made enclosed charts.
Whether you are a first cousin once removed
or a second cousin to some of these people is beyond me.
It's beyond me too
the truth
of the lives my father listed.

First cousin
second cousin
once removed
twice—
it doesn't really matter
where you start
some distances
are too great
to cover
without imagination.

Even Grampa

seems far removed.
I haven't worn
his hunting boots
since high school.
Vacation ends tonight.
Good trip. My father's note
the only English in the leather grasp
of the small Welsh Bible
on my shelf

Evidence that I am
one
in a long line
and perhaps the last of our clan.
On paper, in my father's hand,
lines trace back to yesterday
but those same lines also draw a map
to where the story may end with me.
I am an unlikely means
to the next generation.

Still
I find myself drawn
to river rapids.
I am prone to throwing things.
I shy away from ships in port
and railroad bridges.
Though I've learned to control
my temper
my snoring remains strong
and my thin fingers still get me in trouble.

It is enough to live
with the names of long-ago kin
places inhabited
fish thrown back to the lake
so much is unretrievable.
It is enough to know
what might have been
the ones
that got
away.

Simplifying

Steeped in deep
thinking
a rich brew
of you
I sip
my thoughts
as if drinking
tea.

One UniVerse for the Living

While palaces attest to the power of men,
And monuments mark their wars,
Little remains of the women who've been—
Except for the sons that they bore.
But the voices of women were baked into bread
And later buttered with epics
While the souls of their daughters
Stitched with fine thread
Became tapestries stored in attics.
And all through the ages
Men boasted like beasts
Erecting pillars of marble and stone,
But still they found themselves only to be
Sculpted of flesh and bone.
Philosophers pondered the nature of gods
Outlawing temptations that plagued them
And earning themselves, against all odds,
The power to punish the pagans.
By writing themselves into sacred books
The clergymen sealed our fate
To follow decrees that have their roots
In nothing but misguided hate.
So, children of Adam and invisible Eve,
challenge the wisdom of sages.
Don't be so sure sacred scrolls that you read
Aren't filled with human pages.
Walk in the wilderness.
Eat of the fruit.
Don't let them buy you with wages.
Plant your own garden.
Drink of the wine.
Learn how to be courageous.
Hearts that are hardened
To what is divine
Have honored the dead too long.
Search for the stories
Baked into bread
And eat until you are strong.

The Price of a Muse

I write for
resurrection

to see bodies reassemble
and rise

I've tried to write my dog
off of the pavement

my first girlfriend back
into my arms

a love into more everlasting
than it was

my own soul
into being.

I know now the price
of a muse.

My writing
has not saved me.

It won't
save you.

But let me try
to raise us up.

X. CHOICE

Natural Selection

Thomism: *reason seeks knowledge through experiment and observation, while faith seeks understanding through divine revelation. Thus the two are never in conflict.*

is love rooted in faith or reason? darwin weighed carefully. he made a list of the advantages to marriage. shared expenses. warm meals. companionship in old age. dusted bookshelves. clean socks. mating. a longer and more compelling list of disadvantages. half the closet space at best. the need to be on time. social appearances and expectations. removing the bird specimens from the freezer. financial responsibility. crowding. emotional demands. remembering to put the toilet seat down. no place to put the bones. in the end he concluded that we are all slaves of one sort or another. then set the wedding date and married his first cousin.

Like Kissing Your Sister

For CRB

Lombardi's most loyal fan
you posted his words in your bedroom.
Winning isn't everything; it's the only thing.

You let me tag along
as if indifferent
to my presence
but if someone suggested
no room in the game
for a girl
the look you shot them
put me on a team.
Character in action.

No mercy
once we started playing,
that's how I remember it.
Once you learn to quit, it becomes habit.

Pain wasn't in your vocabulary.
When I broke my arm
you left me in the snow
to carry my limp wrist home on my own.
If you can walk, you can run.

I thought you didn't notice
how much it hurt. I thought
you thought I was faking.
They may not love you at the time, but they will later.

Today, you tell me about
about a hockey player hit so hard
his heart momentarily stopped
mid-beat center-ice.
I expect you to quote Lombardi.

Hurt is in the mind.

Instead you mock the play-by-play
  "He got hit in the chest," the announcer says.
"The chest is where the heart is."
You add your own comment on commentators.
"They all talk too much."

We tease about the way you treat
your dogs, a pack of wide-bodied retrievers
with single-syllable names
who sleep at the rink
eat pucks
and generally fend
for themselves.
I know how much you love them
though you would never use the word
your way of observing
that non-Lombardi rule:
Do as you would have others do unto you.
Confidence is contagious.

I have grown to admire
your brotherly way
of loving
what he called *heart power.*
I have stopped thinking
of your distance
as indifference
and I can generally fend
for myself.
A tie is like kissing your sister.

I think about the guy
whose heart paused
on the punctuation of a cross-check
as I watch you in a game of pick-up.
The oldest on your team.
Fatigue makes cowards of us all.

With a heart

that hasn't skipped a beat
in forty years
you take command
of the puck
and Fatigue cannot catch you.
The ice still brings your passion
to a prominent forefront.
You are not indifferent
on skates.
You do not keep your distance
from the toothless forward in front of goal.
It's not whether you get knocked down;
it's whether you get up.

You always knew
how to say more
by saying half.
Run to daylight.

Your life remains
a Lombardian lesson.
Like the man himself
who commanded others
gap-toothed and
grinning wide,
the intensity in your eyes
dares others to follow.
Don't look now,
but between your tough
and your tenacious,
your tenderness
is showing.
Winning is a habit.

Entertaining Possibilities

"Why sometimes I've believed as many as
six impossible things before breakfast."
—*The Queen of Hearts,*
Alice in Wonderland

riding bareback
on a triceratops
through green galaxies
while you ride beside me
on your favorite mastodon

running a finger
over those I love
and like a highlighter pen
turning them neon
noting them forever
so I can return to them
easily
when I need them

thinking something good
can come
of "ethnic cleansing"

swimming in an ocean
deep and wet enough
to fill the eternity
of love
between these two
sheets

walking into the vowels
of a word like *open*
and becoming it

locking away
Pandora's box

putting evil back
in its place for good
and swallowing the key

lighting myself
with a single match
then watching me melt
warm and liquid
over your body
cooling gently
in the shape of you

sitting flat
in round anticipation
I will be page 233 in the book
that you have just opened
and I will chew on each delicious moment
of every turn
as you move
page by page
closer
to me

stowing away
in your pillowcase
and sailing on your dreams
so that when you are sent to walk the plank
I can catch you
together we can be
the mutiny
on any bounty

letting my best ideas ripen
beside yours
on the vine
then stomping it all juicy
between toes
yours and mine
aging
then bottling it all
till the sun falls

and we uncork
our store
one by one
and drink
forever in the twilight

planting a memory
watering the spot
watching it grow
tall, tender, familiar,
then putting my ear
to its blossom
and hearing
my grandmother's voice
tell me
again
that I can be both the gift
and the giver

The Source

They find their way
through the blinds
and lie down
beside you
every
morning.

Thin airy sheets of
light
inching their way
across your long sleepy body
sweeping away
the night

they fill the room
with daybreak
then follow you
out the door
pushing your shadow
ahead.

When you turn
the beams look you in the eye
your shadow darts
to the other side
trailing behind you
smoothly matching your every move.

They call you
to mountain tops
to open spaces
to the edges of earth
to watch their
dazzling descent.

So let me enter
them.
Let me be fire and burn.

Let me be the center
around which the earth
turns.

Let me ride the red shift and solar winds.
Let me be the blaze.
For if the rays of heaven
will shine on you
why not let those fingers of light
be mine?

Stow Away

How will we know when we have overstayed
our berth?
And God saw the earth,
and behold, it was corrupt.

I haven't my sea legs yet
but I am ripe
for the command.
"Make yourself an ark of gopher wood."

Not every bilge rat
gets so clear a mission.
"I will establish my covenant with you;
and you shall come into the ark."

So why not stow away with me
on this random rolling vessel
as rain and the end of the world
pour down upon us?

Come into the arc
of my arms.
Behold. This is one way
to drown.

Why assume
in this millennial wave
that the captains of industry,
though greedy enough to amass empires

and rich enough to arm fleets,
will be the ones
who rise above the rough streets
chosen and charged with the prophetic task?

"How many cubits?"
you ask
and my only answer

the unspeakable covenant

of love.
In the wake of this flood
we will repeople the earth
two by two.

But who
and when
and what
is the vision?

To what new equator
will the trade winds blow?
What cargo is there to cherish
and store below?

Hoist up and What ho! The release of the anchor
will free us, my brave buccaneer.
Make yourself as understood and seaworthy
as any gopher wood.

All hands to their stations!
This rattling battleship
is under command of the hungriest
and the loneliest hearts.

We shall turn on the wind
navigate by the stars
in your eyes
and trust this rusty tiller to its own whistling whim.

Who can say
that we are faithless?
After forty long days
and forty warm nights

we'll throw open the hatch
send forth a dove
and see what promises
come.

Love Fragments

All things were together.
Then mind came and arranged them.
—Anaxagoras

Let the fragments behind us remain.
    Then name what cannot be healed
        in the hope that time's heat
            shall seal the open wounds.

Nine muses are too few
    so accompanied by this flute
        or by nothing at all
            sing on.

Who said that you were small and ugly?
    Why leap from the Leucadian Rock
        for the love
            of a sailor?

Oh, you exhaust me,
    my white-robed Aegean woman
        bare thighs peeking through to me
            from behind the robes of Iona.

Loosen your folds
    pour your indigo eyes into mine
        and give rise
            to your clearest, most liquid, voice.

Oh, Corinna!
    Did you really take Pindar on?
        What shards of truth and women remain?
            Which of their verses on tablets endure?

This city state has gone mad.
    Tell me again
        how Periander killed Melissa
            and ravished her delicate corpse.

He buried her
    without burning her robes.
        Oh, let me gain strength
            from her suffering.

Her spirit returns now
    to complain
        of the cold,
            So Hera calls us to her temple.

She charges us to strip ourselves
    pile our best clothes high
        and burn burn burn
            for Melissa.

What else have we to sacrifice?
    What else shall the fire consume?
        Whose turn is it to burst with song?
        Where is Periander now?

When the burning is complete
    when the air no longer stings with the odor
        of hot flesh and hair
            bring out the best of the seers.

Let the entrails be scoured
    for the better half of an hour
        to find what omen rests
            in the perineum.

There may be more reliable sources.
    There may not be.
        But let the oracle be heard
            in more than the wing beat of a bird.

Teach me to taste your rapture
    to capture the depth of your shadow
        to read and rupture your pain
            to name the parts of you that remain unnamed.

How does one hold back restraint / retrain inhibitions / restrain the reflex to protect /
    curb the dog within / hold back the urge to hold back / arrest that stray desire
    to stay / strain against the freeze of fear / let loose the runaway train /
    let loose / learn to rain / just rain rain rain

I have known the sound of failure
    heard its rude cackling
        at my worst and slightest mistakes:
            a mocking misstep or the echoing of an all-out error.

I think about Athens
    and Georgia O'Keefe
        the playground, your whirlpool, the eye of your salty storm.
        When is the sacrifice complete?

Where is Periander?
    Who will comfort Melissa?
        Is Hera still listening?
            How will we pick up

Where we left off
    where we left
        where we
            where

I miss the commute
    Route 128
        paved anticipation
            of arrival

Lined with longing
    the pavement
        slipped smoothly and swiftly
            beneath me.

St. Francis knew the bear
    to be born formless
        licked into shape
            by its mother.

So too
      were pagans licked
            into shape
                  by religion.

Bear with me
      my love
            what a conversion
                  it has been

To be
      licked
            into shape
                  by you.

"To write a thought
      is to distort the heart
            of the idea"
                  says Socrates.

Just in case he is right
      there will be no love
                  letters
            for you.

Devotion

I have watched the flight of a shrike
with such devotion
that no god could withhold from me
a branch to perch upon
in heaven.

I have let the sweep of sorrow
rake me, overtake me, turn my stillness to dreaming,
rechannel the flow of my blood stream.
I have felt the vast sliding of something
gliding past the round corner of an eye.

I have been the torrent.
I have let the tumble of it all
run off with my marrow,
leaving me bone dry and bruised.
I have gushed and poured, eddied and oozed.

I am the vacuum abhorred,
the lion's roar and the death of a salesman.
Through it all, I have remained equally
awed and adored by the flood and the drought.
I have gone weeks on a diet of nothing

but doubt.
I have harbored calm
and ambushed rage.
I have aided and abetted
spiders.

I have shouldered the cold
and the crooked
chanted along with the wet Om of the rain.
taken vain revenge on storms—an eye for an eye.
I have been fed with the river's fork.

Yes, peace is sometimes edible.
Sometimes heavy.

Always polite.
It will sit anywhere
but only if invited.

And I have welcomed that quiet
into my bed. Asked her to lie beside me.
I have flirted, seduced, teased.
I have pleaded with peace
to be my wheezy companion.

She has asked so little in return
and I have obliged.
I have befriended trees and trespassers.
I have sometimes lied and often learned.
I have put some fires out, leaving others to burn.

Having had only this earth
to live, to forgive
and to believe in,
I have faithfully worn the habit
of my own skin.

Don't Look

Oh, to be a lover
laced in the coil
of a flying cow's tail
or to be soaked
in an oil-stroked sunset
and serenaded by rooftop roosters

I raise my lips
to the peasant skies
and kiss Chagall's villagers
hello and good-bye

In their eyes
the promise
that love
makes all
possible

A blue-faced cow
with dainty step
and upturned brow
tip-toes at play
and winks my way
then smiles to the rickety rooster
who cock-a-doodle-doos
under the watchful tick tock
of the canvas clock
and soon
as boy and girl
artist and beast
I have entered the cobalt sky
and let my parasol provide
the benediction of a bird-shaped shade
protection from highway-wide brush strokes
that cascade on my bouquet of rhyme

I am my own parade
step-stomping

through a fiction sky
on time time rosemary and time

Oh, cling clang
bing bang
and tum tum tum
to pound the drum
to sound the bell
to unleash the cries
to be the very note
on which
all else
relies

Sing on
painter and painted
don't look beyond
the pitch of the roof
don't name the man
under your hoof
just keep the brush
alive

Modern Sainthood

If only the gods
would confess
to us
what it is
that they require

Then we could
retire the ancient book of saints
those lives marked by simple
assignments:
part the sea, cast out the snakes, turn blood to roses.

Shall we look to the future
or to the past
to find a present
path
to sainthood?

How safe is it to assume
that doomsday
will be broadcast live
or on tape delay
without commercial interruption?

So what glimpse of the everlasting
can this present hold?
How much penance can one pay
in a world that extends
such long lines of credit?

I say a prayer
to our Lady
whose lips are sealed,
keeper of secrets,
Saint Tupperware.

Hooray for Saint Velcro
who watches over

those of us
who do not trust
permanence.

Nourish us, Holy Twins of Peoria:
Saint Anorexia
who keeps herself finger thin
too meatless for the hungry wolves
and men

While her sister
Saint Dorito
consoles the hunger of others,
canonized
for empty calories and brand loyalty.

Bless us,
Saint Duct Tape,
holding the hapless
together
in spite of ourselves.

Who among us shall
be called
recalled
uncalled for
or simply canceled by some sacred Neilson rating?

How much farther do we have to fall
before wine turns to water
and the bread itself
is nailed to the cross
unable to rise?

I can see in your eyes
that you believe
in a tarnished trinity.
We hold these truths self-
fulfilling and inevitable: money, spin and bigotry.

But who today can name their own sins?

Who said that the meek
shall inherit anything
or that you need
breast implants?

And to the Republic
four witches stand
ready with abracadabra spells
stirring their patriotic brew
of barley, hops and all that we slew.

Heal thyself
as you make love-
the-sinner-hate-
the-sin mockery
of other people's lives.

Oh, the holy
are unwhole among us
in high-rises
alley ways
and at the dry cleaners.

The patron saints of
paper clips
Post-its
and polar fleece
offer what little relief

Is left
in this crumbling
of everything
except
denial.

Just give us this day
medicinal marijuana
to calm one ounce of the suffering.
The terra firma
inhales beneath us.

Don't look now
but mothers are rolling
in shallow graves
trying to change the pale names
on their headstones.

Go ahead
keep knocking
on unlocked doors.
Even pigeons scoff
at our altars.

The terminal keyboards
we bow to
daily
and the clerestory that holds
the gore we call the nightly news.

Genuflect
in the end zone and smile.
Read the Gospel of
Dow Jones.
Then stand safely single file

Awaiting the wafer
nourishment green
from the waterless font
our baptismal
cash machine.

Pray that Saint Rayon
will keep us warm.
Ask that Saint Nuclearbomb
protects us
from harm.

If Saint Nick of Time
cannot save the tired
the hungry the poor
(as Liberty
certainly cannot)

Then Saint Air
of Nike will promise hope
of a faster mile
a longer throw
a higher score.

If you must confess
look into the camera
enunciate clearly
on tape
and lie lie lie.

Like high priests and presidents
deny all.
No revelation
in this nation
ever begins with the truth.

This is America
after all
where the fall
reoccurs
every day.

So far beyond original sins
of settlement
are we
that we have forgotten
our need for redemption.

In a world gone insane
how does one obtain
something as sacred
or as intangible
as survival?

The Chippewa knew
and the buffalo too
to beware
the copperhead hiss
of the snake-eyed preachers' arrival,

A shake and a promise
on one hand
and on the other
crossed fingers
behind the back.

The only promises kept
were the ones they made
to themselves.
Oh, holy paperwork
piling up on the shelves

layered with apathy
and mold.
What is there about
squeezing through the eye of a needle
in a land where the camel is a brand of smokes?

Who has witnessed
the traitor's kiss?
Who knows the bliss
of a holy hoax,
or how to resist?

Having feasted
on bitterness
brine and betrayal
what sweets awaits us
in our graves?

Screw
stew
spew
or chew life
to the bone.

Let the hollow of a leg
be the relic of an hour
past and devoured
by something
other than time.

In this age
of caste
and cast off
only our rage
will save us.

Dressed to Live

Today is my newest garment.

Let me put it on
with ceremony.
Let me step into the day
as if to bathe in the passing hours.
Let me tuck in the loose ends
with precision.

Today is my newest garment.

Let me wear it as if it holds
my head high,
as if it can carry me
on its shoulders,
as if it will protect me
from the howl.

Today is my newest garment.

Let me fill my pockets.
Let them bulge with riches:
light on the wide sidewalk,
kind words from a stranger,
things perched, newly born,
carefully placed, aging gracefully.

Today is my newest garment.

At night
let me disrobe
grateful and whole,
knowing that
tomorrow
I will dress again.

Printed June 2000 in Santa Barbara &
Ann Arbor for the Black Sparrow Press by
Mackintosh Typography & Edwards Brothers Inc.
Text set in Giovanni Book with Skia titles by Words Worth.
Design by Barbara Martin.
This first edition is published in paper wrappers;
there are 200 hardcover trade copies;
100 hardcover copies have been numbered &
signed by the author; & 22 signed copies lettered A–V
have been handbound in boards by Earle Gray.

Photo: Lise Shelton

Born and raised in Massachusetts, NANCY BOUTILIER currently lives, teaches, learns and loves in San Francisco. Her first book of poems, *According to Her Contours,* earned a Lambda Literary Award nomination in 1992. Boutilier considers sneakers the highest form of shoe life, and the pen remains her weapon of choice. She considers physics an art form and poetry a science. The only dreams she can recall are those that she has while awake. She generally trusts gravity, even when she is falling hard, fast, and headlong. She believes in magic.